The 101 Insights

FOR YOUR PERSONAL & SPIRITUAL GROWTH

PHIL WALMSLEY

ISBN: 1-4392-6492-9
ISBN-13: 9781439264928

*Dedicated to
the personal God that lives within each
and every one of us.*

There is always choice.

Contents

Introduction

The Insights are about my questioning mind. I tend to question many things but I have an especially inquiring mind in the area of philosophy and religion. Questing for the truth is important to me. Many times, I have found what I thought to be a permanent truth only to realize after receiving more information and having more life experiences, my so-called permanent truth was, and is still being, surpassed by another so-called permanent truth.

Thus, I realize my search for truth, my search for who I BE and for God is evolutionary. My received truths have not been via a blinding flash of light or any other kind of extra-sensory, revelatory, mind-blowing experience. My truth is realized through the persistent searching and consistent listening for answers. This searching, questing, and the sum of my life experiences to this point in time are where and who I am at the time of writing this book. After reading this book, my truths and perhaps your truths will have changed.

The 101 Insights were bestowed upon me one Insight at a time. All the Insights were preceded with my questions based on what was happening in my own life experience. I cried out for help. I will share with you a bit of my personal history that led up to this "crying out." To do this I need to go back in time, a time when my life was in utter chaos. I was recently divorced. My former wife made a different life choice and neither the children nor I figured prominently in her future. I began raising our four children on my own. This was a time of financial despair and emotional upheaval. To be sure, I felt abandoned. I felt abandoned not only by my wife, but also by God. "How could God let this happen?" I questioned. I thought of myself as a good husband and a good father, surely I deserved a better fate than to suffer the painful words of, "I don't love you anymore." While I was distraught at my wife's exit, I was even more distraught that the great loving God of mankind would be so cruel to me. Why me? I can remember saying to God, "If this is the way you make friends you're going to be a lonely person."

While I may have been angry with God for his lack of concern and abandoning me, I did not have a lot of time to dwell on such. Putting myself aside, I made it my mission to raise my children, then aged between two and seven years old, and to assist them in seeing life as a pleasant journey. They too greatly suffered by the disappearance of their mother. We banded together and I became both mother and father (I wore no dresses). Life struggled along in many ways especially financially. It was one thing for me to be struggling emotionally, but when compounded with financial stress, it felt as if I was completely abandoned.

A couple years later, a long-time lady friend chose to be my partner and assist me in raising the children. It was at this point the Insights began to come forth. I believe my ability to hear my inner guidance was due to the heightened awareness and energy that came with the combination of my emotional struggle and the emotional high of being in love. While I cannot say for sure it was not simply a coincidence, I believe the juxtaposition of these two events, triggered the Insights.

One sunny fall morning my long-time friend, who was now my partner, and I were lying together in our bedroom when I felt a presence. I was not sure if I should be afraid or feel exalted. I felt this presence move around my room. I was in a bright room. I could not see any visible signs of this presence. I do know I wanted to speak out and say, "If you have something to say, then say it." Being somewhat nervous by this presence, I decided to put on a bravado façade. I spoke to my partner, Ruby, and calmly said, "We are not alone." She became apprehensive, even fearful and the presence quickly disappeared. (The emotion of fear creates a low energy vibration and this level of energy stops the ability to receive a higher energy vibration of guidance).

Once the presence was gone, I had a tremendous urge to write. I didn't know what to write, but I did know I wanted to write. I couldn't wait to sit and write.

Later that evening, once all was quiet, the opportunity to write did come and I picked up a scrap sheet of paper and prepared my pen. As soon as I positioned the pen over the paper, the presence returned. This time the energy was much stronger. I was not fearful; in fact, it was quite a calming presence. That's one thing I had not felt in quite a while: myself calm. There was no apprehension; I allowed the energy to be. I felt a tingling sensation in my spine. The best way to describe it is as if a cool breeze was blowing over my back, tickling me up and down. It was subtle, yet definitely noticeable.

I started to write whatever came into my head. What I wrote really didn't sound like me. It didn't sound like me because I didn't have these kinds of thoughts. While I was certainly questing for truth, I always thought it would come in a blinding flash of glory. Here I was, sitting in a chair with a pen and paper feeling as if I was being dictated to; it was not automatic writing. No one was controlling the pen or my hand. I could stop at any time and if I wanted to, I could have never written a single word. But, inside my head were all these words and sentences that needed to be written. I didn't know what words were coming next. I remember sometimes I would hear a sentence, not like it and decide to change it. At times, I did not agree with or understand what was being said in my head, and I would change the wording so it made more sense to me. When I did this, the presence, this energy stopped and my mind went blank prohibiting my writing. Only when I deleted my version of the sentence and went back to the original sentence did the presence come back and the writing continue.

Now understand when I say, "I heard a sentence," I was not hearing voices, it was more like I was thinking quietly, yet what I was thinking did not seem to fit my usual thought patterns. It was as if I were capable of new thoughts, higher thoughts. Eventually the presence would stop. As the energy stopped so did the desire to write.

Afterwards, I would mull over what I wrote and each time I knew I received a gift, an Insight to assist me not only with my spiritual questions but also with ones that are more practical. Often, these writings pointed out where I personally deviated or when I made less than loving (trusting) choices. These writings gave me a point of view, a thought, which could, if I so chose, allow me to move in a different direction. Sometimes it was as though I received a solution, but the solution would be useless if I did not take any action. In all these writings, I was always given choice. Not a right and wrong choice but rather a choice of thought or action in which I would be supported, no matter how confused I might be by making that choice. In these writings, guidance seemed to indicate I was to make a choice because then there could be movement (in what I was experiencing). Sitting in limbo, it seemed, was not a good choice.

This is how all the Insights were written: First, I would have a life experience, and then I would receive the Insight. The presence would sometimes come involuntarily. Sometimes it would come upon request. Sometimes it did not come, no matter how much I asked. There seemed to be some synchronicity between my asking and the presence knowing if it was appropriate to respond. Perhaps I needed to experience whatever it was I was experiencing for a longer period or at a stronger level before the Insight was given. I know not why, but I trusted the presence and whatever the reason for the timing of the Insights, I believe it was for my higher good.

After a period of two years, the presence ceased and I no longer wrote. I tried to muster up the presence but it was just not there. I tried to write as though it was there, but the writings had no energy and no life. They were concocted, uninspired writings. Eventually, I stopped trying to write and let it be.

In 1996, the World Wide Web began to come alive and I thought to myself, "Why don't I take the highlights of these writings and make them into little cards people can see." I wanted to share my gift. I was a bit hesitant, fearing religious people would give me negative response to these Insights, but those fears were unfounded. Over the years, I have received

hundreds of emails thanking me for the Insights and the cards on the In-
ternet. I have had ministers and preachers ask permission to use them. I
have had people, who have been searching for an answer to whatever it
was they were asking, find their answer. I believe in the Insights. They
may not be the "be all and end all" but I do know they have assisted many
people in seeing life from a different perspective. People, through reading
the Insights and allowing the words to bring out their own personal truths
and provide guidance, have had the opportunity to see possibilities where
before they could see none.

People asked me if they could buy the cards, so I made them into a
deck of 101 cards and sold them. I have heard from groups that use them
in their healing circles and from others who wake up and choose one each
day to read.

People asked me to explain the cards in more detail and so this becomes
the next chapter for the Insights. At the time of writing this introduction,
(2008) it has been twelve years since I began to feel that presence.

The presence has returned from time to time but only comes when I
have struggled with an issue and exhausted myself in the experience of
discovery. Does this mean I have the answers inside myself at other times
and only need to listen?

As you venture into *101 Insights* know they are written in the order
received. They are chronological. If you study them, you will see the issues I struggled with and perhaps still do. I hope this book assists you
with your own personal and spiritual growth. May this book bring you
one-step closer to knowing yourself and your Creator, the God source that
lives within each of us.

The truths contained in the Insights are wholly personal. I claim these
truths as MY truths because that's what they are. I offer these truths to you
and you may or may not accept any of them as your truth. If one of MY
truths feels right then accept it. If it does not feel like your truth, this is
fine. Find your own truth.

I thank you for choosing this book and hope it serves you well.

Preface

101 Insights is a compilation of "inspired" insights. They were given to me at a time of what I called desperate emotional struggle. At the risk of not wanting to appear selfish, I thought they best be written for anyone to view. While they are highly personal in nature, they speak to everyone. *101 Insights* is a journey through my struggles and how the God within me was ever guiding me to find the light I didn't even know I had.

In *101 Insights*, there are answers to questions about money (in my case lack of money), love relationships, commitments, destiny, secrets, sex (wow! Who would have thought the God within would talk about sex) and many other subjects/issues I have come up against. Each Insight is a new and revealing way to look at life.

101 Insights will have a profound effect on your life. (Well maybe) Those who have read them report life-changing events. Just ask my editors. *101 Insights* has been online since 1996. I receive many emails thanking me for making them available. Now they are available to you in this book.

A quick thanks to those who assisted me in writing *101 Insights*. I hope this experience changed their lives for the better. The following people spent hours with me editing (and believe me editing my work is no easy chore): My wife Ruby Walmsley, my daughter Sarah Walmsley. The first real effort at editing was by Wendy Hickman of Minnesota followed closely by Tanara Bowie. Special thanks to my final editor (and a great blessing), Wendy Mamoon. " I found the greatest gift through reading Phil Walmsley's *101 Insights*, that being serenity and self awareness of who I am and what I can do, Be and create when I am truly connected to my "God". This self-realization spurned confidence to help others and myself, I am inspired to change my life and know it is me, who must change. God willing, all people who read this inspirational work will be so changed their lives become what they want them to be and peace and love abound in them, as it is in me," said Wendy Mamoon of her experience reading and editing this unique compilation of Insights.

Thanks also to Steven Schneiderman of Tulsa, Oklahoma who created the book jacket. He also assisted with and continues to assist with the promotional text for the 101Insights website.

A special thanks to the higher power who believes in me and has faith in me, while I blindly struggle. I know this same power has the same faith in you that is has with me.

The only reason this book took so long to write was lack of intention. That lack of intention has now been transcended by the willingness to commit.

Phil Walmsley

Insight #1

STRENGTHS

Be proud of and use your strengths! The lessons you have chosen to learn in the past will serve you well. They were necessary. They made you aware of the helplessness and despair humankind can take on. Will you show others there is another way? You have enough lessons and truths inside you to touch each heart with love. Let those who encounter you see your magnificence! Touch every heart with love.

In most people's lives, and probably yours, there are great and difficult challenges. Those challenges result in much emotional struggle and turmoil. It is from the pain of these struggles, if we change our perceptions, we see we are presented with an opportunity. If we look close enough and let go of the pain and emotional drama, we are able to see what the experience taught us. What feels painful, threatening, and uncomfortable is able to transform us and lead us into developing or recognizing our strengths.

Personally, I lived with an alcoholic, sexually abusive father. While this was not all who he was (he did have positive influences in my life), this was the painful part and the part that required me to bring forth my strength. Those who know about sexual abuse know the focus is not usually sex; it is about power and control. I learned early what it felt like to be overpowered, given no choice, forced into unpleasant situations, and to have someone manipulate me into doing things I did not want to do.

As a young boy, I recognized the lack of choice or freedom I had in this situation. As I matured in age, I made a conscious choice not to copy the abusive actions of my father, but more importantly, I made a choice never to force anyone to do anything they didn't want to do. (My children may argue this fact, as they recall numerous times I "persuaded" them to eat their vegetables.)

The point of this Insight, the very first Insight I received, told me I could (if I so decided) take what seemed to be a loss of choice in my life and turn it into something else, an attribute representing my strength. I wondered to myself how many other people had experiences or were having experiences where they felt they had no power, no control and no choice. How could I possibly teach people there is a way to let go of all this anger, hate, and feeling like a victim? Is there any room for love in place of control and anger? How can I show people *Love* is the only way out of this pain? Who am I to think I have the wherewithal to bring this message of love to others? Here I am, a man who has stifled my past, buried my emotions, now innocently writing my first Insight, and being asked to speak of love. I confirmed to myself that I know so little about love. My strength to BE was challenged to emerge from my perceived pain of the past. Could I turn my pain into strength?

Then as coincidences go, I read a short story; it went like this:

A man looked out into the world and saw despair. He saw the starving millions and the brutality of war. He saw the devastation of nature and the selfishness of man. He wondered why this was so. One day he was so overwhelmed with all he saw, he got down on his knees, pounded his fists into the ground, and yelled at God. He yelled loudly with tears of anger running down both his cheeks, "God there is so much hate, so much crime, so much killing and you don't do anything about it. Why don't YOU do something about it?" Much to this man's surprise God responded, "I did do something about this... I sent YOU."

This one short story called me to BE.

The urge for me to present myself as a person of love became a driving force. I chose to help others. I did not know where to begin. I had enough problems just coping with everyday matters never mind trying to solve the riddle of Love. I knew I had, and I still know I have, much to learn about love. I continue to learn. It is a never-ending process and a never-ending joy.

Insight #2

TOUCH A HEART

Many hearts are closed to the love of this universe. To touch another's heart, you must first open your own heart. Not just to a selected few, but for all to see. Be open. Be vulnerable. Allow yourself to be loved and to love all you meet. Take those whose ideals are in concert with your integrity and bring them along with you. Your compassion, gentleness and your love for your fellow man is strength for you.

I believe the reasons for my existence are to love my fellow man, God, and myself. Yes, I am part of God too. You are too!

For me, the way to another's heart is through my own heart. The only way to my heart is through my heart. Surely that makes sense? When I express my spirit, when I express my gifts, talents and experiences I begin to touch other people's hearts.

My gifts; my talents are from my heart. I can usually express my heart, but only to a limited few. The loving part of my self, the God part of me, is tucked away and unavailable for most to see. I am willing to share this part of my self with someone, but only with those whom I have a trusting relationship. This includes my wife, my closest friends, and sometimes my relatives. What would happen if I were to share the God part of me, the loving part of who I am, with everyone? Could I express who I really am to everyone? I cringe at the thought. What would people think of me? Would they think I am nuts? Would my friends abandon me? Would my family abandon me? What would happen if I showed everyone my heart? Do I even know what my own heart is capable of? I can only help open the hearts of others when I share my true self with them. If I can do this, I open the door (or create a place), where others have and feel the freedom to share who they are. When I begin showing others who I am, by being the Loving ME, I attract those who want to open their hearts.

While I am an expert at hiding my heart, I sometimes take a risk and open my heart to others. Interestingly enough, I have never been rejected by anyone I have opened myself to. Truth be told, anytime I have opened my heart and shared of myself from a place of love I have always been amazed at how the people I am with will open their hearts too. It's as if my leading the way gave permission for that energy to be present. Love affects all who are in its midst.

I don't enter into the open-heart relationship with everyone... yet. I do enter into open-heart relationships with people whose integrity is in concert with my goals. There becomes a reciprocal giving and receiving in these relationships. There are people whose hearts are closed and (in my opinion) whose integrity is not in keeping with where I am going. I give no energy to and do not enter into relationships with them. One day I will have the courage to open my heart for all to see. One day, I will rise above myself and have the courage to open my heart to those I judge as not being worthy to deserve my open heart.

Touching another's heart begins by expressing my love for all to see.

Insight #3

CHAOS

Letting go of the chaos, the business (busy ness) of the physical world allows a means to see the higher vision. Take time for yourself. Not just a minute, or a day, but a month. Take time each day to be still and listen. Start looking for your higher vision, your higher calling. Remove yourself from those areas where you find struggle. They are a distraction. Move on. Relax. Enjoy life. Enjoy living.

All of us experience chaos in our lives. Chaos feels like life or events are moving faster than we are. We pick up the pace to keep up with what seems like an endless stream of crisis or demands on our time. Our lives become a whirlwind of activity. Our minds become overloaded with things to remember that we forget some of them, which leads to more crisis, more chaos.

I am an expert at creating chaos in my life and must be constantly aware of falling into the chaos trap. I like to think I am pro-active, a person who is creative, and completes what I set out to do, I am someone who takes action.

Can I stop the chaos routine I create on automatic pilot? Sometimes I literally bounce around like some sort of lunatic, thinking because I am so darn busy I am making some sort of progress. Aspirin can be the order of the day. Food is a nuisance. I don't have time to eat! The kids are annoying. "Just go away, I'll be with you soon." The bills will be paid tomorrow. Doesn't that phone ever stop? There is no doubt I feel I am carrying the world on my shoulders and I feel responsible for this world. If I could only stop!

This Insight suggests my chaotic life could be so much easier if I only took time to listen to the little voice within me... that ever so tiny voice urging me to be still, to be quiet, to relax - to take a time out. I did not give this voice much attention. I was having enough trouble just keeping up, so slowing down was not an option. I did not see how slowing down could assist me in any way. Meditation drove me nuts. I know many people love meditation, but for me ... well I have things to do... I just can't sit around for any amount of time quieting my mind. I want my mind to be busy so it can come up with some great idea so my life becomes easier... then... I can actually slow down.

I took heed of the Chaos Insight in spite of my doubts, and over a period of months, I began to take more and more time for myself. It was just a little time at first and I might add it was uncomfortable. It felt more like I was wasting time and I was already pushing what seemed like 25 hours a day. Letting go of the chaos, the quieting of the busyness meant the dishes were left unwashed. The laundry may not have been folded (never ironed) or a host of other menial, trivial, and time-consuming things were not completed. I began to let go of areas where I found myself struggling. I stopped ....ok, maybe slowed down a bit, believing I had to do it all myself. Letting others assist me was part of this process. Whether in business, personal relationships, money, or work, I began to think, "I am more important than this chaotic mess I created. I choose to let go of this and find an easier way." I realized I had created a reality where I must do everything. I seldom asked for assistance in any area because I felt stupid or incapable if I did. So I struggled along in many areas, trying my best, trying to do it all myself. How foolish. By doing this, I did not enter into relationships with other people nor did I allow others to express or show their talents, their gifts to me. Accounting is not one of my strong skills. So why do I fight with bookkeeping? Why not hand that over to someone who enjoys bookkeeping. I am not very mechanically minded, so why not allow someone else who enjoys this type of work, to do it for me. This was part of my learning to let go of handling it all.

After sitting quietly (not meditating) and just relaxing, by just being quiet, my stress load was reduced. I found I was far more receptive to new, fresh, exciting ideas and opportunities. I switched from an "always in a rush, always in a drama" kind of guy, to a more relaxed, easygoing observer. In essence, I became a watcher of energies, rather than dancing in the whirl-pool. By removing myself from the chaos, my energy increased. This was a surprise! I expected to become lethargic and lazy, but the opposite was true. I began to have new ideas, new revelations, and new ways of seeing people and opportunities.

Chaos is a great way to keep ourselves so busy we do not have time to realize there may be another much easier way. If you find your life is one of chaos - Stop! Take time for yourself and listen.

Insight #4

COMMITMENT

The struggle is not about lack of commitment from those around you, but rather about your commitment to your own life. The level of commitment you see in others mirrors your own level of commitment to yourself. Commit to that which is in line with your life purpose, your life's work. Some of your commitments are nothing more than wishful thinking. Everything you are committed to having, you already have.

Say I AM COMMITTED TO HAVING... AND MEAN IT!!

At times, when I look around I see a lack of commitment in other people. From where I stand, it appears people are not committed to their lives. People talk incessantly about what is right and wrong with the way they do their lives; I see a lack of action. I fail to see what I call, "being committed to [his or her] life." People set goals, but there is no commitment to seeing those goals realized. It seems more like, "Please God, now that I have said what I want, could you, like, deliver it soon?" I am increasingly frustrated with people who are not committed to being who they say they want to be.

These people are a mirror for me, a reflection of myself not committing to my own life, my own life purpose. Yes, I have my life purpose in front of me, but in truth I was saying, "OK God, you and I both know my life purpose, now just make this easy for me and I will do my thing (life purpose)".

I only attract what I commit to. When the last statement made was, "Everything you are committed to having, you already have," I asked myself, is this all I am committed to? Surely, I can commit to more. Surely, I can do more and be more committed to my life purpose than this.

The commitment (or lack thereof) I see in others, is not about them, but about me.

Insight #5
CHOOSING LOVE

You have chosen to enter into this plane. This was your choice. Your angels have been with you all along. They whisper into your ear. You have heard them many times. Now is a chance to choose again. You have a chance to choose love, for this was your original purpose. You have come full circle, and yet you are only at the beginning. For there is no beginning and no ending. **Choosing love is the highest choice.** *Become more aware of the forces that surround you. These are powerful forces that call you to "be," and will assist you on your journey. You are not alone!* **There will be whisperings in your ears. Listen.**

Wow! Did I really choose to enter into this plane? At first, I thought this writing was about me choosing to come to earth. Some people believe we are souls flying around waiting to choose our parents, our family, our lives, our obstacles, our tribulations, and our victories long before we are born. I am not a big proponent of life being prearranged or predestined. I do not support, although at one point in my life I did, the concept of reincarnation.

This Insight is about me choosing to raise myself to a place of Love. The plane spoken about here is not choosing an experience on earth, but rather choosing to enter a higher plane while on the earth.

In each of us is the seed to choose love. It is part of us when we are born and it never leaves. We are all endowed with the seed. The seed I am referring to is the instinctive desire to be in a place of love. We all desire to give and receive love. My original purpose, my first yearning was to experience love. I don't think that has changed.

I found during, and since, writing the Insight cards, I have become more aware of forces and energies around me. I am talking about higher forces, those most people would term an angelic or uplifting vibration. These energies, these beings, are willing to communicate with you and me to show us higher ways, if we are willing to listen. You can choose to listen to yours.

Do you find yourself yearning for love? Perhaps you have forgotten you yearn for love? Choose love. Choose to love on all levels, in all situations. This is the highest calling any of us can answer. Be love. Be loved.

Insight #6

PUPPET

Do you think the Universe has nothing more to do than make you a puppet for its amusement? To watch someone (you) fail? The Universe is committed to love. You are asked to give love and the Universe responds. Do not get caught up in self-glory, or controlling or manipulation of others. Be of love, compassion, and grace.

At times I have felt, and even now sometimes I feel, my life is akin to me being a puppet. It seems God or a higher universal energy is taking some sort of sick pleasure in making my life as difficult as possible. It appears no matter what direction I take, it is the wrong direction. Sometimes I see light at the end of the tunnel, only to have those hopes and dreams dashed away from me.

I wonder if I am being tested to see how much I can endure. I wonder if I am paying for past mistakes. I wonder if there is any end to the failures I encounter. Why is God making this so difficult for me? Is God so blind he cannot see I need a break? Is he so blind not to notice I am weak with exhaustion, weak in spirit? Does God somehow find it amusing to watch me suffer? Does He want me to go down on my knees and say, "OK, YOU win! I don't know what you win, but you got me beat!" Then will he raise his hands in victory, and pat himself on the back? Will he whisper to others who can hear, "Ha! I told you I could break him?!"

This Insight tells me God has no such plan to beat me into submission. God is a God of love; God has no desire to see me fail. What parent would ever want to watch their child fail? Would you manipulate your child into failing and expect in return that they would love you more? No.

The universal energy or God has no desire to manipulate or control me, nor does He want me to fail. Yet, while I may fail or perceive I have failed at certain tasks, it is merely my perception. It is the significance I put on my experience that causes emotional stress.

The Insight asks I become a person of love. Asking me to become a person of love has its difficulties. I don't believe I understand love very well. The walls and blocks I must face to see and be a person of love seems insurmountable. I am very good at creating frustration and anger. These walls of anger and blocks of frustration come in many forms. They may be physical or mental. I may need to let go of old relationships, old ways of thinking, and old habit patterns. I must choose to let go of those self-created negative thoughts that support me in not being the loving person I want to be. By moving ever forward and upward to a place of higher love means leaving behind those people and things that do not help me accomplish being a person of love.

No longer do I want people in my life that support and agree with my self-destructive thoughts and actions. I want to surround myself with positive, spiritually uplifting people.

I must change my thoughts so I know I come from a place of love, compassion, and grace and so I know God and the universal energies are supporting me. I am not a puppet on a string for God's amusement. I am a child of God, ever moving toward the love of my Creator.

Insight #7
BE PROUD

Time to let go. Time to be free. The chains that hold you are about to be released. Do not be afraid. Step forth and be proud of who you are. See the world as though every part of it is an extension of who you are. What is showing up for you? Love? Abundance? Joy? Do you believe in your own abilities? Why do you keep them to yourself? A good hockey player would look silly if he just played in the rink by himself. Who would marvel at his speed and agility? Whom could he inspire and become a role model for? Are you playing in the rink (the arena of life) by yourself? TIME FOR YOU TO SHINE!

Be Proud is a very important Insight. I constantly remind myself of this because Be Proud is about showing my gifts and talents to others. Seeing the world as though it is an extension of me is a hard concept to grasp. What does that mean, anyway?

Here is the way I interpret it: Whatever happens, whatever I attract, whatever I choose is an extension or part of who I am. Whatever happens in my life, family, business, or recreational activities is an extension of where I have placed my thoughts and the choices I have made. In plain English (I wonder what happens if this book is translated and this sentence is still here) I CREATE MY OWN REALITY. It makes me accountable for where I am and who I BE in my life. By looking at what I have and what I am creating, I can see who I am being. My thoughts and actions create my manifestations, my life experiences, where I am physically, mentally, financially and spiritually.

The manifestations are the life experiences I attract to myself and they are reflections of who I believe I am.

I continue to stress to you; all of us are unique. We are all created equal. Since birth we have made different choices, chosen different paths, and had different life experiences. Because of these individual choices, we acquire for ourselves gifts, talents, and skills. We excel in some of these skills.

For a number of reasons I often hold on to my gifts, talents and skills, but do not share or show them to others. The hockey player analogy works very well. Can you imagine the great Wayne Gretzky never playing hockey because he did not want to show others his "gifts"? The world of hockey would never see his great skills, although some of his opponents might be glad. I wonder how many children Wayne Gretzky inspired and still inspires and who now want to learn how to play hockey? How many children have put on skates, picked up a hockey stick, slapped a puck around, and experienced the joy of the game just because this man showed them his talent?

It is easy to look at Wayne Gretzky or any other famous person and say, "Yah, if I had his/her talent I could do the same thing, but I don't, I just have _____ and _____ as my talents.

What is your gift, your talent? What gifts or skills are you pretending not to know about? I think you know. Think about it. Each one of us has our own gift or gifts. I do mean everyone. You do not have to have the talents and skills of a Wayne Gretzky. Whatever your skills, you have the ability to be of service to all whom you meet. If you are able to speak in front of a room full of people, maybe you could be a public speaker or teacher. If you are a writer, search for how you can best use your skills. If you have a beautiful voice, sing or teach someone to sing. If you are a homemaker, take care of your home with pride. The point is to do what you know in your heart to do and do it well, for all to see.

When you share your gifts with others, you receive more experiences that are positive. The breaks will come. What you have been seeking or asking for - will come. Would that be love, joy, and financial abundance? The fastest and easiest way to attract goodness is to share your talents and the joy it gives. The more you share, the more people will be attracted to who you are. The more positive you become, the easier it is for you to attract positive people and experiences. Share with pride, grow, and receive. And so it goes.

Do not conceal a gift or talent you possess. Now is the time to let it out and let it shine.

It is time for you to shine.

Insight #8

NOISE

The noise, the confusion, is all a distraction you create to pull you away from your purpose. Notice when the noise is too loud; it is a sign you are off course. The noise prevents you from listening. Have you noticed the volume seems to be turned up? You must be still and listen to hear the whispers of your spirit guides. When they speak loud, the volume of the noise and confusion, in your reality, increases. The noise increases proportionally to the whisperings from your spirit guides. This keeps them out. Choose a quiet time each day to be still and listen. Choose a quiet time to listen.

My life is often one of noise and confusion. This is when I know I am off course. I am not following who I "BE." I am not living in harmony with my goals, dreams, and purpose. An increase in inner and often outer noise is a sure way to know I am out of sync with my higher self.

Noise can be many things. Noise can be the people who I surround myself with or those who seem whinier, rowdier, and angrier than usual. Noise can be the cry of a baby that sends me over the edge. Noise can be from the TV or radio that once seemed friendly and now seems to agitate. Noise can be a phone call from a friend or, even worse, the bill collector.

Noise prevents me from listening. Imagine two sides of a conversation. Each side has an opposite view. One side is shouting in your left ear, the other side is shouting in your right ear. It is difficult to hear just one side. I surmise it is my beliefs and thoughts yelling in one ear and my inner guide yelling in the other ear. It is difficult to hear just one side and discern to which message I should be listening.

The louder the inner guide speaks, the louder the thoughts seem. The only way to hear my guides is for me to be still, to quiet my noisy belief system, and give audience to the guides. This requires I give 100 percent audience to the guide; it is easy to hear when I choose to be quiet. The act of being quiet does not mean I must light 101 candles, burn incense or sit in a difficult or uncomfortable position. Being quiet means just being quiet. It is about focusing on the voice within rather than all that is on the outside. It is making a conscious choice that I be aware there are whisperings in my ears and knowing I can choose to pay attention. As I listen, I become attuned to them, for they offer me new awareness that leads to new and higher choices.

Be Still and Listen.

Insight #9
THE SPOKEN WORD

The spoken word is very powerful. It carries a vibration. The spoken word reaches the Universe and is returned to earth magnified. Saying you "can't" or "that's impossible" will come true. Believing something is possible also returns magnified. Choose what you want. Do what you know to do, then, and only then, will the next step be given. You must do the work. This is to be joyful. If it is not joyful, re-examine what you want. After you have done the work, let go and let the Universe work with you.

The spoken word is powerful. It has more power than speaking in your head. It has more power than writing. When I speak, the words carry a vibration that is energy. This energy is real. It is carried to the universe and it is reflected back to ME, magnified.

When I have negative verbal conversations, I find my life in constant struggle, dealing with things and happenings I consider negative. Do I put others down? Do I gossip and make fun of others? Do I express a constant barrage of anger? Do I use negative reinforcement? If I speak of myself as a failure, the Universe supports me in creating my failures. My mind is my creator. When I project "I am a failure," that energy attracts all sorts of happenings in my life where I get to prove myself right. I attract what I really believe. My thoughts, words, and actions create my reality.

We are truly our own worst enemy. The creative energy or God does not withhold from us. This energy, by way of our spoken words and daily choices, is more than willing to support us. We are what we say we are. We are what we believe we are.

When I have positive conversations with others and/or myself, I project positive energy. I will find my life receives constant blessings and positive happenings. If I project the energy of a positive person, positive happenings are returned to me. It is that simple. What I believe and speak is what I get. By looking at where I am, I can tell who I am being.

Science has described this as mind over matter.

I speak my thoughts in words every day. I need to be aware of and watch my conversations. Do I speak higher thoughts? Do I speak well of those around me? Do I consider my conversations with others to be uplifting? I must be aware of conversations I have with others and of their conversations with me. I can choose not to participate in negative conversations. When speaking with others **I always** believe one should attempt to converse at the highest possible level. Is it possible to talk to, and about others, with kindness, gentleness, and true love for them?

When I speak, I must learn to speak from a place of love.

Insight # 10

GIVING AND RECEIVING

Always look at the purpose. Why do you choose to give or not to give? Giving is about reaching, working toward, or being in harmony with your purpose. Receiving is about accepting being in harmony with your purpose. They have the same results, yet come from different sources, and yet are from the same source. They are one. To have difficulty in either giving or receiving does not allow you to move forward. It is shutting the door. Allow others to give to you without keeping a chart of how much they have given or how much you must repay.

There is the skill - to <u>give **and** to receive</u>. Most people are not balanced in this area. They either give much more than they receive or conversely they take much more than they give.

It is important that those people who are "givers" understand if there were no "receivers" they would not be able to give. There must always be receivers and givers for giving and receiving to work. If there are not any givers, there cannot be any receivers.

Giving and receiving is best when done with a purpose. The purpose of why one gives is more important than what one gives. Giving, when coming from a higher "God-like" intention is well thought out, unselfish or without a self-serving reason. It is given freely with no thought of reward.

Likewise, receiving should be the same way. It should be accepted with joy, with the spirit of the higher intention, received with no thought of keeping score as to how much was received versus how much one may have given.

Giving and receiving are equally important, but true giving and true receiving always come from a higher place; a place of love.

Insight #11
GIVING AND RECEIVING

Accept receiving. You cannot give unless you can receive. You cannot receive unless you can give. The energy is the same. If you ask people to give or if they just choose to give to you, know it is not your responsibility to repay them. Through the Law of Abundance, know the Universe will repay them. When you give, give all, for the Universe will repay you. It is all about the energy. Giving allows others to receive. Receiving allows others to give. It is a circle, a cycle, and a continuum. You can choose to break the circle or to keep the energy flowing.

Accept receiving. I have difficulty being in the receiving position. I prefer to be the giver. When I receive love, money, compliments, joy, or anything positive, sometimes I can feel very uncomfortable. My personal belief system prevents me from receiving. When I am given compliments, I am often embarrassed and I make jokes to quash my feelings of discomfort. Sometimes I respond with a compliment of my own. Adoration or feelings of affection are even more difficult to accept. While I must admit I do want to be feeling love, when it comes, I find myself having difficulty receiving it, absorbing it, enjoying it. I wish I could joyously accept the gift and just say "Thank you."

I cannot give unless I can receive. I cannot receive unless I can give. The energy is the same. It is like a circle. Both elements of giving and receiving are necessary to keep the flow going. This keeps the circle moving.

I have been taught it is better to give than to receive. I say, it is better to give and to receive. I have been taught it is selfish to receive. That just doesn't make sense. If no one is receiving, no one can be giving. There must be a giver and a receiver.

After receiving, the ever present ego voice in my head asks what I must give back to keep it equal. The stressful exchange of Christmas presents is a fine example. Is there not a mental accounting of how much to spend and on whom? If Aunt Mary always buys me the most expensive gift, must I spend more on a gift for her as compared to what I spend for others on my gift-giving list?

When I give to someone, I do not expect to receive anything back in return. I am quite happy giving to them. Why then, can I not accept that when people give to me they might be quite fine with giving to me, just as I am fine in giving to others?

The Universal Law of Abundance is about just that, abundance. I need not keep score of how much I give or how much I receive. The energies of giving and receiving manifest. When I give out of love and joy, I will find many opportunities to receive love and joy. When I receive out of love and joy, I will find many opportunities to give love and joy. And so the cycle goes.

Giving all does not mean I put myself in an unhealthy position. It is about giving without scarcity playing a part. If I have $10.00 and want to give $5.00 as a gift and I feel great about giving my gift, this is good. The Law of Abundance repays me many-fold. If I give $5.00 away afraid I will not have enough, I attract scarcity. I am sure to lose my last $5.00 dollars. While the action is the same, the thought process and the beliefs behind the action create different results. My belief system is more powerful than any action I take.

I make myself aware of opportunities I have to give and to receive and notice my emotional response to each. I will begin to notice how I give and how I receive.

Insight #12

DISTRACTED

It is easy to deceive yourself into not completing your life's task. It looks easier to wander off the path. Oh! How easy it is to be distracted. How easy it is to listen to those who say they know better, to those of authority. Listening to those who "have made it," is so attractive. To be helpless, useless and to give your power away in hopes someone will show you the way, someone will carry you and make it easy. This is when struggle appears. Shake off your fears. Replace them with courage. Have the courage to love those who desperately wait for you to touch them.

I find it so easy to be distracted as I make my way through life. The most distracting part of life is life itself. There are so many vices that can lead me astray. I find myself searching for pleasure. This pleasure is not a wild abandoned pleasure. It is the simple pleasure of recreational activities. I work every day so I can enjoy recreation. I work so I can create a life of ease. Is that paradoxical? There is nothing wrong with seeking pleasure until it becomes addictive and all consuming. Pleasure is destructive when its energy becomes self-serving to the point of being selfish.

I imagine myself living a life of ease similar to those that appear to live in the world of pleasure. There are those people who seem to have every-thing they physically need and want – in abundance. These people speak out and I listen. I crave to live without the constant battle for funds to meet bills. I crave for the experience of just being frivolous (without guilt) without creating financial damage to my family. Oh how I wish I could just be rich and do what I please. I wish the constant struggle would end and some rescuer would save me from this merry-go-round (not so merry) of financial responsibility.

Sometimes I listen to others who appear to know all the spiritual truths. It may be an individual or an organization that speaks certain truths to me. I want to have the experience such a person or organization has with their perceived freedoms and their desired lifestyles.

I want someone, who appears to have spiritual knowledge, to lead me. I want someone to carry me, to make my quest easier. I say to God, "God, just tell me what you want me to do and I'll do it." (But I have to be sure it is God) How do I do that?

This Insight states, while we may wish for a spiritual know-it-all and desire God to come forth from the heavens and leave us a direct unmistakable convincing message, there is only one way to find our path.

Our path is one of choice, the choice to love one another and to love God. The choice of doing God's will, which is to love God and to love each other. Loving God is not easy because it is love chosen by faith alone. When choosing to do God's will I must be of the highest service to my fellow man. It is about taking action and making my choices reality. There are many people who long to see, hear, touch, and believe, in God. Can I be true to myself, hear my inner longings and listen to my God within? Can I rise above my fears, my pursuit of pleasure and have the courage to BE the LOVE I so much want to share? When will I let go of the pleasure seeking rewards and begin the inward journey to finding God?

When I reach this point: the point where I let go of material desires and the belief my success is measured by material wealth, I can allow the joy of service to reign over my personal desires. It is said this is all the pleasure I will ever need.

Other pleasures are certainly welcome, but I have the choice never to let them be a distraction from the pleasure of service.

Insight #13

WHISPERS

OH! How the voices of our reality receive so much more attention than those guiding whispers that speak softly in our ears. Take time to be still and listen, for we are always guiding you.

Inside me is God. Not the whole God, but a piece of God. This God piece is not there to record my every mistake (that would take up way too much of God's time) or to taunt me that I am walking a road to hell. This God-part is an actual part of God; it is a fragment of God. This God-part follows all my choices. It allows me free will as well as doing everything within its power to assist me in moving closer to God. Yet, this God-part in no way ever makes a choice for me. This God-part of me, of ourselves is always there, available to communicate with us. All we need to do is listen.

There are voices of my reality. What is the voice of my reality? It is what my logical brain perceives to be a truth. This can be a person, newspaper, television show, psychic, book, religion, parents, friends, neighbors, or children. These are all voices of my reality. They exist. When these voices speak, I listen in a logical way. I process the information given. I store and often use the data for present or future decision-making purposes.

The voices of my reality speak loudly because they are always present within me. There is a constant inflow of information, a continuous bombardment of my reality. I was and still am, taught to be logical, sensible, and responsible. I look at flow charts, crunch numbers, and listen to those voices of authority. I make logical, sensible, and responsible decisions (sometimes). In a sense, I am a computer. I file this here and that there until everything is in its right place.

The voice of God is an opportunity to listen to spiritual reality. I could choose to take time to sit and be still. If I take time to stop and listen, to tune into, and become aware of those quiet whisperings that assist me on my journey to peace and love, I find logical, sensible, responsible decisions may give way to those whisperings that are intuitive, uplifting, and exciting. Listening and acting on the God-voice, results in the expression and fulfillment of my Spirit. I will take time to be still; my God is always with me, always assisting, always supporting. Always.

Am I willing to communicate with my God today and every day?

Insight #14

PATIENCE

Patience. Forward patience. You can move forward even when waiting. There is great change and preparation taking place. Be patient. Look at the struggle. Be patient and wait, knowing you have done all that is currently required. No need to waste energy on what is already in motion. Go forward into your vision, without moving. Let it be.

Remember Insight # 2 – Chaos? The one where I saw myself as some sort of lunatic bouncing around in life. Now I get a patience card. Like I have patience... not. I felt to move forward, I must be constantly on the go and forever in motion. "Idle hands are the work of the devil" may be the message playing in my head. Maybe all I need is to practice forward patience.

Forward patience feels excruciatingly slow, like nothing is happening. I want to tap on the window of the Universe and say, "Hello, is anybody out there?" Patience is boring. But, patience is necessary. On this earth, we have a reality of slow motion manifestation. We have no choice to practice patience all the time. Driving our car from point A to point B is a lesson in patience. We are not capable of instant manifestation. What if we only had to think we were at point B and we arrived at the same moment as the thought? (Might save gas?) A chaotic thinker like me would never be able to stay in one spot for more than a few seconds. Thank goodness that doesn't happen! I'd be all over the map! If all of our thoughts manifested instantly it would sure be chaos.

The concept of forward patience is to trust what I have set in motion is going to manifest. When I cook soup from scratch, I perform the action of gathering ingredients and preparing them for the soup. I prepare all the vegetables, slice, dice, and leave some whole. I choose spices and add them to my soup. How does forward patience come to play when preparing soup? It's when the soup is on the stove cooking of course. I am now practicing forward patience. Everything is set in motion and I must wait for the soup to be ready. It must be cooked. Other than the amount of heat I give the soup, I have no control over how it cooks. I alone cannot cook the soup. I cannot hold it in my hands and cook it. I must allow a tool to help me make (manifest) my soup.

In my soup of life, I gather all the vegetables and spices and, sometimes after much procrastination, I decide to make soup. I put the ingredients into a pot, turn on the burner, and the soup begins to cook. However, at this point I do not practice forward patience. I stop the cooking process by taking the soup off the stove, changing the vegetables and spices. Then I put it back on the stove to cook. This cycle of beginning to cook, then changing the recipe, is repeated over and over again. Constantly changing my recipe-of-life will leave me hungry. I tell myself I am "doing" all the time, but nothing manifests. I have no manifestations because I keep changing the recipe. I never let the soup cook long enough to manifest. Choosing vegetables and spices is like making life choices. Gather your ingredients, take action; put them in a pot. Finally, allow time to cook. Wait for the results!

This is forward patience.

Insight #15

PATH OF GOLD

Open up. Relax. Have fun. Life is about joy. It is not meant to be a struggle. Sit back and create what would bring you joy and happiness. What would energize you? What lights you up? Be honest. Feel it. Now go for it. Have it. It is yours. The Universe is a supplier of requests. It makes no judgments. Ask and you shall receive. This is a Law. Asking is planting a seed. Receiving is sowing the same.

Asking for those things in line with your life purpose gives you results because they are in line with your purpose. If you are on your path, everything flows. If you ask for things not on your path, struggle ensues.

The events that have happened in my life seem to me just that – they happened. I certainly did not believe I had a lot of control in these events. I definitely was not conscious, in any way, of creating my reality. How could I? No one ever taught me my thoughts, desires, and intentions would result in a … result. I knew things happened. I thought more about God either blessing me or tormenting me based on what happened during my day. I went from acting like a child to an adolescent to an adult, from one stage to another without really controlling it or doing it on purpose. I remember owning my own landscaping business. I started the business because I saw an opportunity for financial gain. I had no inspiration to be in, or run, a business about landscaping. I had no knowledge of plants, trees, flowers, or grasses. I became a landscaper because the opportunity was there and doing so provided me with an income. I was about 21 years of age during this time and while I worked hard, it gave me a short-term way to earn a living but not much else.

I ask myself, "Wouldn't it have been better to choose what I really wanted to do in my life and then go for it?" At a later point, sometime in my 20's, I decided I wanted to become a photographer and I set about to become one. This was an improvement from the landscaping business because the desire to become a photographer became a passion. I became passionate about becoming a professional photographer. Twenty years later, I am still a professional photographer. However, the desire is waning. I now desire to make myself more useful to people around me. I have passion to be of a greater service. Some of this passion is sated doing photography, but I also desire to assist my fellow man through writing.

I am stuck though, because I don't have the courage to have vision. I don't have the courage to ask myself what it really is I, definitively, want to be or do. I don't get in touch with myself to know what moves and motivates me. If I could but get in touch with my inner self, that God part, I know I could muster the courage to move forward and bring this into my reality.

If I am purposefully in line with my inner self and my passion, I can only succeed. While there is no real wrong path, the path of being true to my spirit and my inner most desires, allows the quickening of manifestation.

When I am inspired, moved, and consciously choose a direction, I attract those coincidences, happenings, and awareness' that allow me to move along my path of choice with far greater ease.

When I make a choice and am committed to that choice, something always shows up to assist me in seeing the manifestation of that choice.

While my life may be a struggle, it is certainly lessened when I am on purpose, focused and in touch with my God spirit.

What lights you up? What gets you motivated? What excites you? What makes you shine? The purpose of what excites you, the underlying reason for the motivation, is key to your success.

Insight # 16

STRUGGLE

A struggle is taking place because you know inside yourself; you are off your path. There is a constant effort by your spirit guides and by the Universe to guide you to your path You can choose the path paved with gold. This is the one where you work in harmony with your life's purpose. Another choice is to crawl through the muck and struggle and fight with yourself to the point of exhaustion. This is the path that shows up when you do not work within your life's purpose. Which way do you choose? **Path of gold or path of struggle?**

Struggle is a sign something is not quite right, something is out place. It is informing me there is a block. Usually the something not quite right, is me. I am off my path. I have certain skills and talents. When I express my skills and talents, I find life runs more smoothly. I feel better about myself. If my skill was painting and I work as an auto mechanic, I might find life to be a struggle. If my skill is working as an auto mechanic and I find myself forced to paint, I might find this to be a struggle.

I keep moving forward by discovering what motivates me, what excites me. When I move forward, I honor my being and myself. Sometimes my sense of BEING gets lost in the DOING.

One of my goals is to let go of the attention I place on physical things and actions. This is so I might see what my mission is, what I could choose to give, see, and understand. My personal opinion is we are only here to learn how to love. We have the choice to learn how to love God, others and ourselves. That is the bottom line.

When I am off my path and I ask for things or experiences, I do receive them. The problem is, those things and experiences do not do anything for me. They only hold a temporary satisfaction. Sometimes the things I receive seem way out of line. The fact my vision and path is unclear to me, leaves a space where "out-of-tune" stuff shows up.

If I am way out of line with my life purpose, struggle shows up. However, struggle is just a sign I am out in left field somewhere. Struggle could easily be changed into opportunity, if I would stand back and ask, "What is this struggle about? Where am I out of line with who I am?

When my body is sick it tells me. It becomes weak and sore and I have pain. It tells me something is not right. My body is in turmoil. So it is with the spiritual body. When the spirit is sick, conflict and struggle take place. The sick spirit is constantly being guided (notice the word guided and not the word controlled) by one's higher self to pull itself back to its path. My higher self continually feeds me information from which I can choose to make a new decision. There is no judgment here, just continual cheerleading to assist me in moving along and growing.

I can choose to fight and not listen to my higher self, my intuition, and that "knowing" part of me, but I will continue to struggle along. If I enjoy conflict, upheavals, chaos, pain and suffering (**by the way I don't**) this is the route for me.

If I can choose to honor my spirit, express and share who I am, I will find my path paved with love, light, and higher learning.

Insight #17

TURMOIL

Be still and look at the turmoil. The physical manifestations before you are a result of your own inner turmoil. You have worked hard! Allow yourself to play, to relax, and to feel all the pleasures of life. The joy and the happiness. Play and play often, for it brings you much joy and this is wonderful.

If I create an inner world of turmoil, I will surely create an outer world of turmoil. If I can create an inner world of peace and contentment, I will surely create tranquility.

As I hurry through the business of life, I often am caught in the turmoil of life. Let's face it. Life happens. So many occurrences and incidences have happened to me. At times life seems overwhelming. I have so much to do and so little time to do it. I must handle this and handle that until I feel like some crazed demon running loose. I always have more things to handle in a day than I have time to handle. I must make choices about what will be done and what will not be done. I seem to be wrestling with too many choices much too often.

When my real world, my waking world, becomes full of real world turmoil, I should know this is because I myself am full of inner turmoil. What issues am I wrestling with? Where am I not physically, mentally, or emotionally free? What am I avoiding? What have I not dealt with? (As if I need more to deal with). The outer turmoil I see manifesting is because I have inner turmoil.

Why don't I take time out to play? Why is it playtime can only come after all work is done... and work is never done? I am not able to play. I do not take time out for fun. I do not give myself permission to experience happiness or joy. I plod along carrying the heaviness of my accumulated life dramas that drag me down so low joy and happiness seems unattainable.

I must choose to allow myself to play. Play for the fun of it. Play! Play! Play!

There are a zillion ways to have fun. Choose some. Then do them.

Insight #18

ABUNDANCE

Abundance is something created, not rewarded. You create your own abundance. Focus on the positive, the abundance. Let go of worry, anger, fear, and frustration. They only chain you. They drag you down. They prevent you from accessing abundance. This holds true for any area of abundance where you feel there is a shortage. The path of gold is created from the inside. It does not come from the outside. It will not manifest on the outside, until it is in the inside.

Does the following sentence sound familiar? "Be a good little (boy or girl) and you will get a..." As children, most of us were rewarded when we did something "good" and punished if we were "bad." Many of us hold on to that memory. We believe we are rewarded when good and punished when bad.

"I helped the old lady across the street, and a bonus check came in the mail for me. God must like me."

"Today I swore at the old lady crossing the street and a few minutes later I fell and twisted my ankle. God must have been angry with me."

I used to believe the better we are - morally, the more we will receive abundance. I believed my financial success was linked to a reward from the Universe or God based on whether or not **I had** been spiritually "good."

Abundance or lack of it, is something created by me and me alone. If I could but stop playing victim to the economy, government, new world order, mail, my spouse, children, environment, job, house, family, relatives, banker, business partner, chakras, soul mate, horoscope, health, and so forth, I will have the capability to create abundance - I repeat, abundance is created. It is not a reward.

Abundance is relative. I may have very little and feel abundant. Could I have a fortune and still feel I do not have enough? Sometimes I struggle just to meet the basic necessities of living. Why is it other people have an abundance of money and I do not? It's just not fair.

I have come to believe the amount of money or love a person has in their life is directly proportional to how much they value themselves. Ouch, that hurts. It places scarcity or lack of abundance squarely on the person experiencing scarcity. I try to create a better life for myself by manipulating my environment. For example, I move or change jobs, change business locations, and still abundance is an issue. I do get results from these changes, but they are not as high as were my expectations. What gets in the way?

Many of you know I am a professional photographer and enjoy photographing weddings. One summer I photographed a wedding for a couple I knew did not have much disposable income. I gave them a very good deal. I charged a fee much less than I would normally charge. At their wedding I stayed longer than the contract stated and I used twice as much film (digital cameras were not available at the time) than originally agreed upon in the contract. This was my way of giving to them even more than the price discount. Prior to the wedding I had to contact the couple several times to collect all the funds they owed me. They had trouble making the small payments but did manage to pay me in full.

When they received their photographs, including the negatives, they quickly went to a photo lab and had many reprints and enlargements made. I know this because they went to the same lab I use. Shortly thereafter, I received a letter from the bride stating how disappointed they were with the photos and requesting their money back. I have to admit I was shocked. The bride complained I took more photos of the groom's side of the family than her side. She complained I only stayed for a certain amount of time when we all knew I had stayed double the amount of time. I did not quite know how to handle this and decided to refund her money in full if she would return all the photos and negatives that made her so unhappy.

She wrote back saying she did not want to give up the photos or the negatives while at the same time she had more enlargements made at the lab. She stated she would settle for a 50% refund. I flatly refused any refund and that is how it ended.

This led me to ponder, "Here I am helping out a young couple, offering them a price break, going the extra mile and they try to take advantage of my good will", what gives? After much introspection, I decided I had shorted myself based on my belief of what I am worth. By undercutting my price and my value, I attracted someone who showed me (and mirrored) my own sense of self worth. I did not give my work or myself enough value; therefore, I attracted someone who reflected this same image.

Later that summer I tried an experiment. I have pricing for different wedding packages I offer. They are geared so the average person would purchase a middle of the road priced package. For this experiment, I decided the next possible client who called would only be offered one package at one price, a substantially higher price than what I currently charged. Well, wouldn't you know it, the bride booked the wedding. I shot the photos and she was thrilled with the results. She wrote me a thank you letter and paid me a substantial tip. She loved my work, was very grateful for my expertise, and loved the finished product.

When I projected the image of "I'm expensive and I'm darn well worth it," I attracted a person who mirrored that same image. They paid me handsomely and were appreciative of my work efforts.

The moral of this true story is you attract what you believe you are worth. This is just one example of how creating abundance begins from the inside. I realize I have in my life right now, manifestations of what I believe I am worth. Whether it is money, love or any other areas where I desire more, I know I am what I think I am, and what I believe myself to be worth.

If I want to attract a prize partner, I had better start thinking of myself as a prize catch. If I want more love in my marriage, I had better believe I am worthy and deserving of it. If I want more money in my life, I had better believe I am worth it.

Issues of, "I'm not good enough and I don't deserve it" allow rich and poor to experience the same scarcity. While the rich may have more money and possessions than the poor do, the energy of scarcity is the same between them. The rich feel poor and the poor feel poor. The same holds true about love. Those in relationships can feel "love poor" and those who are not in relationships can also feel "love poor." The level of financial status or marital status has no bearing on the feeling of love scarcity.

Valuing oneself creates abundance. I must believe I am worth more. I was created equal in God's image. I have the same potential, the same opportunities to create abundance, as does anyone else. I am the creator of my reality. I create my abundance. When I value myself more, the abundance of money, love, and joy will surely increase.

I control my own abundance. Whatever I have in my life right now is perfect for me because that is truly what I believe I can have. By focusing my thoughts, beliefs and energies in a more positive way, I receive more abundance. It is quite simple. If I have scarcity of money, I must look inside at the beliefs I have about money or lack of it.

I use this exercise: I have a conversation with money. I put a $20.00 bill in front of me and have a conversation with the bill (I usually do this when no one is listening. Otherwise, my family members give me strange looks). I listen very carefully to my conversation. Sometimes I tape record it, then listen to it later. I gain some insights as to my beliefs around money. My beliefs appear to be truths. However, they are just beliefs. I can do this exercise for any area where there is scarcity - love, joy, sex, peace, and money. I can change my beliefs.

Scarcity is the manifestation of fear. When there is scarcity, I know somewhere in me is the fear - if I have an abundance of ... the consequences will be... The result is, I keep myself in scarcity because it is the safer place to be. Abundance is the manifestation of love. Being in tune and on purpose with clear intention produces abundance.

The path of gold (also known as the easier path) is first created from inside me. I must give myself permission to have anything and everything I want. My own self-imposed limitations are all that is between abundance and me. I must first create in my mind's eye what abundance looks like. I visualize it over and over again. I ask my subconscious to destroy any old beliefs preventing me from accessing the path of gold. I listen to my conversations. I listen to conversations others have with me. Others conversations generally mirror your own conversations. Can I give myself permission to have it all! When I am clear on what I want, I focus on the joy of having it, then and only then does it begin to manifest in the way I desire it to.

Insight #19

BELIEFS

A belief is stronger than any action you can take. To take an action when your beliefs are really saying something else gives the belief the upper hand, the power. From the beliefs you hold, stem the results you have in your life. Let go of that which holds you. Be secure in knowing all will be provided for you when you "believe" and create what you want. Believe in that which brings you love and joy. Being busy trying to avoid what you don't want in your life, will surely create the same.

I made decisions. I created beliefs. My decisions were made on an unconscious level. These past decisions and beliefs now reside in my subconscious. My subconscious is like a computer with numerous files. Inside these files are the early decisions I made. In the present, each and every time a situation comes up or decision has to be made, I go to the corresponding file and pull up my past decisions. I then respond to that file.

I know a man who makes plenty of money in his contracting business. Unfortunately, he spends it even faster by way of gambling. This gambling is ruining his business, but even worse, he is losing his wife and family. Through the process of hypnosis he discovered (and remembered) an incident where a neighbor molested him as a young boy. The man who molested him asked him to keep quiet about the incident and paid him one dollar to do so.

This young boy in his subconscious combined two things.

1. The molestation act itself, which made him feel uncomfortable and "yucky"
2. The payment of $1

The decision he made (not consciously) was money is yucky. Getting rid of money has lived in his subconscious ever since. Whenever this man earns money, he is compelled to get rid of it just as fast. Anytime he has money, the computer file is pulled up and says, "Money is yucky." It matters not how much this man earns, money will always be yucky. He will always spend it.

His only option is to change his belief. He must overwrite the file. As an adult, he has an option to know the file that was written as a young boy no longer serves him. He can, at anytime, make a different decision around this event. He can remove this damaging file entirely from his hard drive (his subconscious) and replace it with something that serves him. This man, although aware of the belief, chose not to rewrite or recreate his file. He is now divorced, making even more money and in more serious trouble from his gambling expenditures.

If I stay on the same example of money, there are stubborn people (**me**, for example) who rather than change their belief, just bury it. I simply ignore it. I see signs all the time of what my beliefs are around money. To see my beliefs I only have **to see** my reality. My reality is created from my beliefs. Unfortunately, ignoring a belief doesn't work, as the Universe or God is always moving me forward. I am constantly given the opportunity to remove decisions that do not serve me. The only way for these decisions to be removed is for me to recognize them first. I continue to place money issues in my face so I will eventually see them for what they really are (a belief), remove them, and move on. I am accountable for what I attract. As I sow, so I reap. As I believe, so it is. When my subconscious is planting money-wise seeds, it attracts healthy money manifestations.

My non-serving beliefs (and we all have them) hold me in a place that keeps me comfortable because I believe my subconscious file to be right. I wrote it. It must be right!

Now is the time for me to choose what I want, and remove the "beliefs" that prevent me from moving forward. Once the "untrue" or old file belief is removed and replaced with a new, positive-serving file, money or any-**thing** can be manifested differently.

Thinking any of my actions or busyness (such as working harder or changing jobs) is more powerful than my beliefs is simply not so. I must remove the belief, rewrite it, and live (action) the new belief.

Insight #20
LOVE RELATIONSHIPS

Only you have the power to create whatever type of relationship you want! Loving those in relationships are mirrors, illusions you create to further your own spiritual growth. These relationships are not real and yet they are. Will the person you choose be a struggle or a joy? It's your choice. Look at the relationships in your life and ask if they are filled with joy and love. If you perceive them as a struggle, you can let go of this struggle by seeing, focusing on the love and joy. Focus on the positive. No matter how small or how distant it may seem. The more you focus on love and joy the fewer struggles will show up.

What kind of love relationship do I have? Is it the kind of relationship I want? Somewhere I read a line that triggered an awakening in me. The line read something like this: ALL MY ANGELS AND ALL MY DEMONS ARE IN MY LOVER. That sure rang true for me, and judging by the amount of email I get dealing with love relationships, the previous sentence is true for many others.

Our partner, lover, spouse, significant other, whatever we want to call them, is like a messenger sent to us to assist in furthering our spiritual growth. This may be hard to believe when they leave the toilet seat up or underwear hanging on the bathroom clothes rail, but it is true.

I have within myself a belief system. Sort of like a programmed computer. I was mentioning this in the previous Insight. I am the computer and I loaded my own programs. Not all my programs are productive. Some are more like, viruses. They create havoc with my hard drive (my reality). My partner is like a virus announcer. She lets me know when there is a virus affecting my hard drive. How does my partner let me know I have a virus?

Generally, any issue that creates tension in a loving relationship is the sign of a virus. Quite often my partner is mirroring or reflecting my own inadequacies and fears even though it may seem one sided when such a virus surfaces. Both partners, while engaged in a relationship battle, are in effect carrying virus announcements to each other. The trick is to back off from attack mode and look at the virus.

Let's look at an example:

My wife takes issue with me avoiding opening the bills. I know they are there and when I am ready to pay them, I will open them and see they are handled. On the other hand, she likes to open the bills and place them on her desk where she can easily access them. She has dates marked on the calendar when they are to be paid and has set up her auto banking options so everything is paid in a nice, neat, orderly, and compact way.

My wife believes she handles the bills correctly and I believe I handle them just as well. However, this creates tension for us. We could spend a lifetime arguing who should change. We could have numerous arguments over just this one topic. I could attempt to control her to pay the bills my way and she could spend far too much energy trying to persuade or control me to see her way is better. Instead, we use the mirror-reflectivity idea and begin to ask each other, "What is the mirror?" What I see in my wife is a person who is very organized. My belief around her "over organization" is it takes away her freedom. I feel too much of her time is spent organizing. If I go one-step further, my fear is, if I was to be like her, I would be "controlled" by bills. They would be constantly in my face and I don't want to face my obligations all the time. My wife is my messenger. She is showing me my fear around feeling too organized and losing my freedom. I also realize this is not truth. She probably spends less time than I do handling bills, because she IS organized. I spend twice as much time trying **to find** the bills.

I am also a messenger for her. She will be the first to say while she is comfortable with her sense of order and organization she wishes she could have that carefree attitude I exhibit. Her fear is if she becomes care-free, she will abandon her responsibilities and end up having to handle far more details and crisis than ever before. I am my wife's messenger. I show her she needs to relax and play more. I show her not everything has a nice little compact spot. It's OK to let go of control sometimes and just enjoy.

We do this exercise anytime an issue arises, it has helped us understand and accept each other. As a result, I do pay more attention to the bills and handle my money better. I am surely not at the same level she is, but I do see value in being organized. She also understands why I do not want to be as organized as she is. She decided it was OK to come out and play more often. It's Ok to break the rules and eat dessert before dinner some-times. I learned to accept her need to be organized. We learned about our fears. We learned to accept each other. We learned to accept ourselves and be open to the possibility and see the way the other person does life has value.

While attending a personal growth course my instructor asked me to describe the positive characteristics in my spouse or "significant other." She wrote the many words I used to describe my significant other on the large easel at the front of the classroom. I described her as thoughtful, play-ful, sexy, intelligent, caring, etc. Then she asked me to name one thing I didn't like about my partner. I jokingly said, "She always uses up the toilet paper." The facilitator took my comment and drew a black dot about the size of a quarter right in the middle of all the positive characteristics I had mentioned. She asked me to come to the easel and walk up to the black dot. I complied with her request. She asked me to step right up to it. I moved closer. She urged me even closer until my forehead was actually touching this black dot. She asked me what I could see. I replied, "I can't see anything but the black dot."

"Exactly," was her comment, "This is what happens in relationships." Speaking to the rest of the course attendees she lectured, "All these wonder-ful characteristics; warm, kind, loving, he used to describe his significant other... and all he can focus on is the black dot." She got her point across to me, and the rest of the class.

Are you focused on the black dots in your relationships? Take a moment to write down all the positive traits you can find in your partner. This is where your focus needs to be. This increases the positive energy flow between you. When the virus announcers arrive at your doorstep, listen to them, for they have value.

Insight #21

LOVING SELF

As for the love relationship you have with yourself, are you joyful and happy within yourself? Do you feel alone? Do you "need" other people around you not to feel lonely? Do you create chaos to prevent feelings of love for yourself? Do you scatter yourself and your energies so as not to look at your own magnificence? Loving yourself is the ultimate. You cannot love another until you have made peace with yourself. If you have not made peace with yourself, all the people who show up in your life will represent parts of you that require love. These people are sent to you as mirrors, as guides. **Let go of your fears. Access joy.**

It is important I love myself. It is important I honor myself. It is a must I be aware I can play a vital role on this earth and in this universe. I know I can be a perfect light as those around me can be perfect lights too. If I can do these things, I can say I love myself.

Too often in society, we only express our love when we are in an emotional bond with another person. We say words like "Oh, you make me so happy!" While we may feel happy, it is not the other person making us happy. They don't have that power. What is happening is we feel happiness inside ourselves. Why not say, "Oh, I make me so happy!"

It is true when I see troublesome behaviors in another person it is a reflection of who I am. I discussed this in an earlier Insight. The mirror is an opportunity, something I need to address to grow. If this is true (and it is), it must also be true when I see love in another person that love must be a mirror of who I am. That love, while being present in the other, is a mirror of my own love within. The lover is merely a messenger. The message is "I feel love." The mistake I could make is I could believe the other person, the messenger, the lover, is the one responsible for creating my love feelings. I say this is not so. I am the one responsible for creating and experiencing my feeling of love.

My upbringing teaches me; to be whole I need to have a significant other in my life. Everyone seems bent on finding his or her soul mate. I'm not a big believer in soul mates. I believe every one of us is each other's soul mate. The best soul mate you could ever find is yourself. I believe relationships are stronger if two "wholes" are put together instead of two "halves." It is false to think two halves – no matter how loving, make us a whole person.

I know I create chaos in my life and constantly blunder my way along so I will not see my own magnificence. Certainly, I am not worthy of magnificence. My mistakes and selfish ways are great reasons for me not to love myself, or so I think.

I am often surprised I am loved. I think to myself, "If they only knew what dark secrets are within me, they would never love me." Truly, I feel flattered someone could actually love me. Could they actually love me for who I am? Can I possibly love myself knowing who I am? Loving me is not an act of selfishness. It is the only way I know that makes it possible for me to love another person. To be forgiving of my past mistakes and be patient while on my path is to honor myself. To be happy when there is just me, to have compassion for myself, laugh at myself, be motivated by myself and secure within myself is all part of loving myself.

I can create a new relationship within myself. I begin today by affirming I am in Love with myself. Love is a verb. It is an action word. It takes work to Love oneself. The more I work at loving myself the less stress there is in all my relationships. The positive energy of loving myself helps attract those people who have the same energy. People that are more positive show up in my life. I find more people entering my life who are loving. I have great relationships with others when I love myself.

The types of relationships I have mirror back to me exactly how much I love myself.

Insight #22

A GIFT

Why do you doubt love? You have much to learn about love and you have already learned lots. You have been provided with a gift. (The person you are thinking about.) A gift of high magnitude. A gift to each other. You have asked to experience the freedom of love. You cannot experience this freedom until you are willing to let go of the chains that bind your soul. Love is the highest calling. Let go and feel Love for it is all around you. Feel it. Be with it. Speak of the love you have for others. Speak from your heart. Speak it with joy. Let love shine in and through your eyes. Others will remember they too have light and love within themselves.

Each and every person that comes into my reality is a gift. Some relationships I create are easier than others are, but even the most difficult relationships are a gift. Each person I encounter is an opportunity for learning something new. Each person provides a chance to choose differently. They are an opportunity for me to grow emotionally and spiritually. They are a chance for me to experience love. At the time I received this Insight I doubted my love for my new "significant other." Seeing this person as a "gift" changed my whole perception about her. A gift to me is the same as a blessing. It is something I should treasure and so I began to see this gift (this person) as an angel, a messenger, as a person who is to assist me in receiving what it is I ask for, and I asked for freedom in Love. As she is a gift to me, I am a gift to her. It works both ways.

Love is the highest calling. It is what we are called to BE. Love is the reason for our existence and the reason we exist. A statement I heard a while ago went like this, "Loving others is important, loving self is critical." Most of us have heard you cannot love another until you first love yourself. I must confess, I believe this to be true. It would be next to impossible to enter into a loving relationship while carrying a ton of emotional and spiritual baggage. It would be similar to trying to eat a big turkey dinner with all the trimmings while constipated (I hope no one is reading this on Thanksgiving). While the turkey may appear good, the result would be even more painful.

There is Love all around me. I must be open to receiving it. It is there waiting for me. First, I have to become aware of it. I have to become consciously aware of it. I must start looking for it.

Speaking of the Love I have for others was an interesting eye opener for me. I realized I did not express my love for another except in their private company. So, I tried an experiment in which I started expressing my love for my partner more openly. Most people who heard me expressing this love were very uncomfortable, yet envious at this type of relationship. While most people were into bashing their spouses for their perceived shortcomings, I was doing the opposite. I suppose they considered me to be lovesick or in the "romantic stage" of a new relationship. I became very conscious not to "bash" my partner, but rather openly compliment her at any given time.

Being a recreational hockey player who plays two to three times a week, I have the pleasure of sitting around a dressing room with guys drinking beer, having a smoke (not me) and chatting about their lives. It is amazing how many guys verbalize their unhappiness with their relationships. The standard discussion is the males whine and complain about the lack of sex in their relationship. Once, I stated this wasn't a problem in my relationship and the whole room fell into an uncomfortable quietness. Someone cracked a joke about his wife, everybody laughed, and I said nothing more.

That was until a few days later, when two of my teammates phoned to confide in me their marital struggles and ask if I would be willing to assist them. So I spent some time with these individuals explaining how it's important to appreciate what you do have in your life and not just focus on what appears to be missing.

When I speak from my heart, with the highest degree of love energy I can imagine, I become a beacon, a light, and a seer for those who wish to experience what it is in me that I reflect. Trust me, when my light is turned on people flock to me because they too want to experience a higher love.

All relationships are gifts and these gifts should be treated with the greatest respect.

Insight #23

SECRETS

What secrets do you hold? Can you free up these secrets? What do you say about your secrets? When a secret is made, either by yourself or with another, you should be conscious that the energy of the secret stays with those who accept the secrecy. A person(s) often accepts a secret from another person(s). The person receiving the secret may consider themselves to be "special," "privileged," or above others when receiving the secret. Accepting another's secret allows the giver of the secret a way of not dealing with their frailties and fears. By "joining" them in their secret(s), you take on the energy surrounding the secret(s).

Secrets. This was a subject I never really thought about until I received the Secret Insight. There is energy in secrets. I thought to myself, surely, it is better to have some secrets locked away where no one will ever know them and where I never have to be reminded of their existence.

In my experience of being involved and facilitating personal growth courses, I see the power of secrets. Secrets cause withholding of energies. The energy of a secret lies within, stagnates, and ferments.

My secrets have power over me. Could it be I have secrets hiding within me? When I carry a secret within me, the secret has a power, no matter how far or how long I have stuffed it away. Secrets gain their power by what I say about them. A secret is usually kept a secret because if it were let out a consequence would follow. Others would validate my fears of loss, shame, guilt, unworthiness, and the fact I am not good enough. A secret is nothing more than a story. The event, which caused the secret, is real but the decisions I made and continue to make around that secret are false truths.

For example: What would happen if I told my spouse about the affair I am having or have had? (This is just an example) I already have a good idea what would happen. She would feel anger. There would be some sort of an emotional outburst. I would feel guilty, perhaps remorseful, or even foolish. I might even feel angry I chose to have the affair. Perhaps letting the secret out may even cause a separation or divorce. Worse yet, what if my partner confesses to the same?

Let's analyze this whole scene and how it pertains to the Secret Insight. The secret is the affair, which is a neutral event. It has no significance until I choose to give it some. When I internalize and say, "I had an affair and I am so ashamed and guilty," the affair now has significance. I may say to myself, "I am not a good person." Without freeing the secret, the guilt and the shame live within me, for as long as the secret lives. To free a secret, it is important I am able to come to terms with it. I can look at it from a higher perspective. I may think, "What good did this experience do me? How is it hurting me by keeping it a secret?"

I am not my secret. By keeping secrets, I could still play the "poor me" victim role or the "I'm so awful, I don't deserve anything good" role and I would never get on with living. It is time for me to let that go. I choose to let people see who I am. This is easier said than done. I am surprised by how much energy my secrets hold and how much of my perception of what other people will think is not true. Can I share my secrets openly and without restriction?

Letting go of secrets is similar to cleaning a closet. Get rid of the old useless things. When I do this, there is room for new, more positive energy. I know my most painful secrets. When I let go of the energy of the secret being a secret I am truly being me. I can show the world who I really am. I am able to show the real me.

I remember one day I was with my wife, who at the time was not my wife. We were dating and discussing secrets. In fact, we were discussing secrets as a result of receiving the Secret Insight. We were driving down a country road when we both agreed to speak our secrets. I have to tell you,

I was nervous. I thought to myself if I spoke my secrets to her, she would want nothing more to do with me. I went first. It took courage to speak my secrets. I was quite sure speaking these secrets would cause her to flee. Surprisingly, after I finished, she looked at me rather nonchalantly and asked if that was it. Was that it? Divulging this information was serious stuff. This was many years of garbage all coming out in the front car seat and she was unmoved by the whole thing. In truth, she was nonplussed. While my secrets ate away at me for years, to her they seemed rather trivial.

It was her turn to tell me her secrets. I was unsure if I really wanted to hear them. She spoke her secrets and when finished, I too had the reaction of, "Is that it?" The secrets that had been eating her seemed to have almost no significance to me. I wonder if the secrets we have are bigger in our own hearts and heads because of our emotional attachment to them.

Accepting another's secret is not the wisest choice because I could "buy into" or accept the other person's "This is so bad" or "poor me" story. Other people's secrets are not truth, but by accepting their secrets as secrets (keeping them secret), I validate their "stories." When I am asked to accept another's secret I say, "I am willing to listen, but I do not keep secrets". They either run away or share. Mostly they run away and become angry with me because they wanted to transfer some of that weight to me and I refused to accept it. They want to be validated as "I'm not good enough" and I wouldn't play along.

Secrets are an energy drain. Get rid of your secrets. Let go of the guilt, shame, blame, I'm bad, I don't deserve to have good in my life "stories" and clean that mind-closet of old debris. You are not your secrets. You are a soul who can choose to be a powerful, positive influence with everyone and everything with whom you come in contact. Place your power where it truly belongs - with you, not with your secrets.

Insight #24

SECRETS

*Speak of Love and Truth and there will be no need for you to carry a secret. Let everyone who meets you know all of you, your strengths and your weaknesses. Let them see all of you. This will allow them the opening to do the same. **Secrets are a withholding of energy. A withholding of sharing and giving.** When you carry secrets, you attract people who carry secrets. By showing people who you are and removing secrets from yourself, you will not attract those who will ask you to help them carry the burdens of their secrets, but rather you will attract those who choose to be free of secrets. **Speak of love and truth and there will be no need to carry any secrets.***

There is the type of secret where I take on guilt, shame and blame for an event. There is the type of secret where I take on another's guilt, shame and blame for an event. The secrets I speak about in this Insight are somewhat different from the ones **just** mentioned.

The secrets I am referring to here are about withholding who I am, that is, withholding my strengths and weaknesses from others. How comfortable would I be sharing with another that I feel weak or vulnerable in a certain area? How vulnerable would I feel if I were asked to share with anyone and everyone my dreams, visions, and ideals?

I believe many of us have a secret self. This is the part of us we do not want to share with others for fear of being ridiculed or feeling embarrassed. This fear blocks us from opening up to others. Sometimes we choose to show it to a loved one with whom we feel safe, but to show it to just anyone is not possible. This secret self is the part that so desperately wants to be freed, shared, nourished, and wants to grow, yet it is just not safe to do so.

My experiences around opening up to others and sharing who I am have caused me great anxiety. (What will they think of me if I tell them my secrets...?) But, in reality, anytime I have opened up and shared who I am, both my strengths and dreams as well as my perceived weaknesses, I have had the joyous experience of freeing up personal energy within me.

In all my experiences of sharing who I am, those people around me did not laugh; they did not think less of me. On the contrary, they thought more of me for taking the initiative to open up. My decision to share allows permission for others to do the same. When I decide to share my inner self with others, the energy of giving and receiving flows freely between us.

You have the opportunity to open up to others and share who you are. While some secrets are about you being a victim, the secrets I am talking about here are the ones you withhold from someone regarding your victories and future dreams. It does take courage at first to make yourself vulnerable, but it gets easier and easier every time.

When you withhold your dreams, passions, and goals, you are unable to share yourself deeply with another. In fact, it is an act of selfishness. This is a conscious choice. It is like singing in a monotone voice, knowing full well you could sing chords and octaves. You are just choosing not to share this gift with others.

When you withhold your goals, dreams, passions, your life, you attract others who do the same. Before long, most of your relationships stagnate. They become relationships where there is no freedom to share anything other than at a surface level.

Do not be afraid to tell others your dreams, failures, and victories in life. When you do this, others will open themselves to you and share their hearts and souls with you.

Insight #25

THE PAST

The power of the past is real. The power of the past is now. All events happen simultaneously. Your perception of time creates the distance you perceive in forming your reality. All is happening at once. The power of your past hangs around your neck like a weight. You have chosen to let go of this weight (your past) and it shall be so. Consciously choose out of struggle. While this may not seem important or significant, it will create a new energy in you. It will be of assistance in your creating abundance. Focus on the positive things you see in all people. You are entering a new level where shifting will take place more rapidly than has previously happened.

Can I consciously choose out of struggle? This may not seem important or significant, but it creates a new energy in me. It will be of assistance in my creating abundance. When I choose out of the struggle, I enter a new level where shifting (changing) takes place more rapidly than has previously happened.

Here is an interesting concept. I have heard the theory there is no time and space; everything is happening simultaneously. What makes this slightly easier to grasp is I create my own time perception. This time perception then forms my reality.

This Insight suggests the past is not really the past, but the present. My past is my present. I understand my past has power. I have not successfully stuffed my past away. I cannot and should not ignore it. My beliefs, pains, and joys of the past are still in my present. It is only my logical brain that tries to separate past from present. On the soul level, there is no past, or present. It is all the same.

So, the past, that is really the present, can become like a weight around the neck. I can consciously choose not to live in my past. I do not have to 'be' my past. I have to acknowledge it and clean it up. That process can look like forgiveness of others, forgiveness of self, healing relationships, paying old bills, etc. I choose to "be" in integrity with whatever happened in my past. (Or is that my present?)

By becoming more in integrity with my past, I am able to create my present. By releasing the past, I create a new energy to assist me in creating abundance in whatever area I choose.

Insight #26

MIRACLES

Miracles will show up for you, continually. Accept these miracles. Thank yourself for these miracles, for you created them.

Definition of miracle: The manifestation of something better than asked for or perceived possible.

I create my own reality. All that I be, do, and have is a result of my own thoughts, beliefs, and actions. In retrospect, it is easy for me to see how I, when in past difficult situations, brought the situation upon myself. How can I claim to be a victim of the police or the government when I chose to break the rules, when I chose to break the laws? It was I who chose not to pay my taxes. It was I who chose to disobey the road signs that resulted in being caught for speeding.

Is it true the person who has a very poor self-image attracts a mate who is abusive? The person who smokes all their life suddenly plays victim to lung cancer? Are you or do you know of a person who is very negative, controlling, and manipulative? It is true this type of person usually ends up with a large number of life dramas (highly emotional happenings) seemingly one after the other. Like a magnet, a person's focus, their thoughts, and actions attract the same like energies back to themselves.

Are you aware the same - be, do, have, works in a positive way too! The person who holds a great self-image is surrounded by wonderful, warm, cooperative friends. People who eat, sleep, exercise, and play right, have a certain glow. People who help or assist others, easily find people wanting to assist or help them too.

Miracles happen to people every day. Is it just luck? I don't think so.

If it is true we create our own reality, then this must include miracles. While it may seem a miracle fell from the sky and landed at our feet, we alone are the cause and effect of this occurrence. Our thoughts, beliefs, and actions create miracles. Our thoughts are the seeds. Energy follows thought. The miracle is the manifestation of our thoughts and actions. This makes us accountable for the position we find ourselves in throughout our daily lives. When my life is not where I want it to be, only I can make changes to my reality, by changing my thoughts, thus changing my life. Becoming more positive and seeing the beauty, joy, and love all around me, I will surely create the seeds for positive and miraculous manifestations.

I create my own reality. I believe in miracles and have faith they will appear.

Insight #27

LOVE SHUTDOWN

When you "see" someone in a love shut down, know you too are shutting out love in some area of your life. Ask: Where am I shutting out love? Seeing a love shut down is about you, not the other person. Give of yourself. When shut down appears, it is because you are either holding love inside (not giving) or you are not being receptive to another's love. You may choose out of a love shut down by asking for the light. Affirm: I choose love I choose light I choose joy

This Insight was given to me when I was asking the question, "Why is my partner (significant other) appearing to not be giving out any love?" Why does this person who I have seen so warm, so affectionate and loving, now seem so cold, indifferent and distant? This distant coldness was a trait I noticed in other partners I have had. I knew whatever makes women (in my case, anyways) become like this, was a pattern repeating itself to me.

My male friends described this as women's nature. They blamed it on PMS, hormonal imbalance, or said women are just plain bitches. I listened to a man who told me I was too gentle with my partner. I was told I was not being man enough. He suggested, and quite forcefully, I needed to lay down the law and assert my rightful place as King of the Household. I heard I was too sensitive, too accommodating, too wimpy, too gentle, too caring, too...

I thought back to the times I have been dominant, aggressive, and controlling in a love relationship. I have played the King of the Castle. I found relationships built with these traits always ended in a battle for control, with neither party willing to give. Each person became more guarded, more suspicious of the other's motives and intentions. This led the relationships on a downward energy spiral and eventually all these relationships died a painful death. I knew from having a sexually abusive father that dominance, control, and manipulation were not the answer to a happy, healthy relationship.

When I received the above Insight and it suggested to me I was the one shutting out Love, I became somewhat angry. It wasn't me being cold and distant. It wasn't me! How could this possibly be about me? So, I pondered for days about where in my life I was shutting out love. I began to watch, to become aware of my feelings and thoughts in this area. Throughout the days, I began to notice how I felt when someone did something of a loving nature for me. Surprisingly, when someone did something loving for me, I felt uncomfortable. If someone did me a favor, I felt embarrassed. If my partner loved me in a way I had not experienced before, I would quickly change the tables so everything was status quo.

I noticed there were many people I shut out of my love. As harsh as it may sound, I deemed them not worthy of my love. I believed them not worthy of and not capable of receiving my love. This included certain family members and friends. It also included people based on preconceived ideas of who I thought they were, or what they represented to me.

The Insight was right. I was shutting love out of my life. I did not allow love into my life. I did not give all the love I could give out. It was that simple.

I have done much inner work since the time I received this Insight.

I practice letting love in and giving love. Now, I see my wife as my barometer. When I see her in a love shut down, I become aware it is I who has turned the tap of love off. She doesn't need to change. I do.

If you are having trouble giving and receiving love, ask yourself where you shut love out.

Insight #28

TRUE LOVE

It has been programmed into you to give and you do this well. Only you do not give yourself any value. You do not come from a space of always wanting to give love. You just know you "should" love and you have trained yourself to turn on the "emotional love juice." You are not accessing that which is higher. That of true love. True love is coming from happiness, joy, and light. It is similar to walking on air. There is nothing there and yet there is. You get to create whatever you want from this level. It is all-powerful.

I have spoken with many individuals in relationships and there comes a point in most relationships where the couples are locked and blocked. Each person has decided they have given enough and are not willing to give anymore. To each partner, it feels like they give and give and give. However, I say this giving is not from a place of love, but from a place of, "I should, because this is what love looks like".

We believe the more we give, even though we are stuffing the "I really don't want to do this" thoughts away, the more we reap rewards. The emotional love energy is the energy required to perform a "should" instead of a "want." An example would be making love when you don't really feel like it, but doing it anyways, to keep your partner happy. Some of us would consider this a sacrifice. Is this Love?

I say it is not so. The turning on of the emotional love energy time and time again leads to a false sense of stability, security, and love. Why is it necessary to have "shoulds"? What would your life be like if you just asked yourself before every task: "Is this a "should" or a "want?""

If I say no to the "should," what will happen? Have I trained myself to be a person who responds to "shoulds" instead of "wants"?

My life (and yours) has the potential to be completely fulfilling where every act I perform, every chore I do, every moment of my life is filled with joy and Love. Here are some choices around how I beat the "shoulds."

Let's say there are dishes to be washed. (Pretty darned exciting, right?) I have the choice to wash the dishes from a "should" point of view. I don't really want to do them, yet begrudgingly I saunter off to the kitchen, showing my love for my family or whomever, and silently or maybe noisily wash the dishes. Do I sound like someone who is living life with joy? I think not.

Secondly, I could just say "no" and not do the dishes. However, if everyone had this attitude, no dishes would ever be washed. :)

I could make the dishes a chore that makes me feel good. Certainly, washing dishes may not be the most fulfilling of my life's purpose but, I could make a choice every time I choose to do dishes I come from a place of great joy. I could make dish washing a joyous occasion. I could make up whatever game I feel like playing and use it with the dishes. I play dish games. "I can wash these dishes in five minutes" and I have fun beating the microwave clock. I could have a contest to see if I wash more forks than knives. Sounds silly I know, but what a change of attitude from the downer of "having"to do the dishes. The difference between doing the dishes with joy and doing the dishes from emotional love juice is - the way of joy is for my benefit, my pleasure, and raises my energy. The "should" way is a drain of energy, for the only thing I create is a false sense of whatever love looks like to me.

True love is accessing that which brings me joy and only I can choose what brings me joy. This true love is an honoring of me. While the dishwashing results will be the same no matter what energy I put into them (the dishes are clean) the process, energy and passion in washing dishes is what will change my life from plain old washing dishes to an energizing of my soul.

I imagine living where everything I do is fun and brings joy, I am passionate about whatever I choose to do. The only thing blocking me from this is my choice of whether I am going to turn on the emotional love juice, to please another or whether I am going to choose to live every moment with joy - for me.

It's my choice.

Insight #29

SEX

There is no need to stop experiencing this physical, emotional level and wait for NIRVANA to descend upon you. Enjoy the pleasures of the physical and the emotional. They were designed to bring you a taste of joy, happiness, and connection. Do not avoid the higher levels by being caught up in the physical. The message here is there is an even higher love that can be blended with the physical and emotional. Seek this level. Create joy, happiness, and light in your day-to-day life, in every moment.

From my own experience and in listening to others I know much energy is created/expended regarding sexual activity. When I speak of sex in this writing, I am referring to all types of sexual activity. It makes no difference whether it is heterosexual, homosexual, bi-sexual or masturbation. The Insight Card makes no distinction about one's sexual preference.

This Insight was written with the question in mind, if sex is/was performed does that prevent, hamper, or slow down spiritual enlightenment?

I wondered if I became celibate or if I curtailed my sexual drive would I be more pure - more God-like? I wondered if sex was distracting me from a higher purpose. You notice I have not said how often I was having sex. If I said I was only having sex once a year, some people would think it was an outrageously long time to go without. Others would say it was far too often. The frequency makes no difference. It was what I said in my own head. I determined what was too much and that is different for each individual.

Because I asked this question, I received this answer.

It was made clear to me enjoying sexual relations, and I stress the word enjoying, is perfectly acceptable. For me to stop having sex and wait for the shining light of God to descend upon me was my own story and not necessarily the truth. The pleasure of sex is an energy that can assist me and/or my partner in becoming more intimate.

For some people sharing each other in this way can be an emotional awakening in itself. I must add it is the willingness to be open, share, give, be vulnerable, care, love, that takes this experience to a higher level - not the physical act of sex itself. All the ingredients - openness, sharing, giving/receiving, vulnerability, loving AND sex create a feeling of connectedness. Is it any wonder sex, for some, can become addicting? Is it any wonder why so many people shun sex? It is one of the ways humans can actually feel connected or disconnected.

The Sex Insight notes even though the feeling of connectedness manifested with intimate sexual activity is wonderful, we must realize there is more. To believe having a great experience through sex is the be all and end all is simply not true. There is within me the capability to attune myself to an even higher energy source that would bring about the feeling of connectedness, even more so. While it is fine to enjoy sex, there is the opportunity for me to become aware there are other energies I may tap into that would probably make sex look rather dull and boring. (I might find that hard to believe).

I cannot let sex become my God; rather it would be better if I place plenty of God – the loving God - in my sexual encounters.

I can have joy in life by creating happiness for others and myself. I can give my love freely. I can be open to receiving the love of others and live every moment of life with my light shining, radiating outward, and inward. I seek to create harmony in all my relationships, including the relationship with myself. I make sexual intimacy playful, joyful and a loving experience.

Insight #30

DOING

There is not much in your way. The groundwork is prepared. Let no one stop you. Be firm. Be committed. Visualize what it is you want. See the people rejoicing? It's time. Just do what you know to do. Don't even concern yourself with what you don't know yet. Time to stand up and be you. Time to do. It's time for you to shine.

Sometimes I wish I could DO. I prepare the way, but then I do not follow through. I stay in a place of planning. I take no action. I say I want to take action but I am not committed to taking action. I am in a state of perpetual mental arranging of the proper order, the proper steps to reach my goal. My goal seems even more elusive when I cannot see all the steps that will lead me to the finish line.

Refreshing my mind with joy and excitement around whatever it is I want to create, helps. When I see (visualize) the end result, the visualized manifestation helps me feel more empowered. It makes my destination seem more real. It gives me a feeling of probability. The destination becomes possible.

It is important for me to focus on where I want to be or what I want to accomplish and not worry about where I am. My believing that having everything in perfect order before I can move forward will surely keep me in a place of stagnation. My worrying about the journey and the steps necessary to traverse the road ahead will create a manifestation process whereby people or circumstance will surely show up. These people or circumstances will mirror my doubts and fears. They will have me questioning the successful possibility of my project. These people will show me where I am, mentally and emotionally toward my desired goal. If I find negative people showing up, I know I have negativity around my goal. If I have people who are major controllers, I know I have control issues around my goal. If all sorts of drama shows up, I know confusion and chaos is slowing me down; keeping me from my goal. I must be clear and focused on who I am and what I want to create. I visualize the outcome of my creation and the good benefits it will have for others and me.

The next step, as the Insight suggests is very simple. I can move forward toward my goal by just doing what I know to do. I ask myself "What is it I know to do?" Although I may not know all the steps to reach my goal, I always know the next step. When I know what my next step is, I must push aside doubts and fears that enter my thoughts. I am often (OK always) my own worst enemy, imagining all sorts of less than favorable outcomes. Not knowing what lies ahead is part of my journey, my excitement, my adventure, and part of my fear and hesitancy to go all out 100%. I have the choice not to concern myself with what I do not know.

I don't know what I don't know.

Once I take the step forward toward my goal then and only then, is the next step revealed. It is impossible for me to map everything out and walk a self-predetermined path. It just does not work that way. The only responsibility I have is to give myself permission to take only one-step. That one-step is the step of doing what I know to do. Once that step is complete, then and only then, can I move into the space of taking the next step.

It is time for my vision, my dream, and my project to unfold. It is time for me to shine. Is it time I accept the manifestations of my thoughts and energies and let the joy, peace and love of my creations shine in? I am responsible for my own manifestations, my own creations. Everything I have RIGHT NOW is a result of my thoughts and actions. I create my own reality!

I must keep focused on who I am and where I am going, one-step at a time.

Insight # 31

BLOCKS

You can have all you want providing you remove all blocks, beliefs that limit you. The blocks in front of you are small. They seem big because your nose is pressed up against them. Choose to make your life one of ease, love, and joy. No need for desperation and depression. Believe in your greatness. Commit to your greatness. Believe in your ability to create.

I create my own reality therefore; I also create my own blocks. Blocks are what I put in front of myself to support previously made decisions. These decisions, now manifesting as truth were chosen before the age of seven. If at some point in my early years I was told I am dumb and I sub-consciously agreed with this I will always have this block "I am dumb" in front of me. This "I am dumb" block was and will be responsible for many, many problems in being who I want to BE. Every time I attempt something requiring any intelligence my inner voice says, "You cannot do this. You are dumb." Thus, the block is always there. Sometimes though, and it makes sense, some things do get accomplished and it appears I may have outsmarted the "I am dumb program." But alas, this too is an illusion. It may appear I have beaten the block, but the voice will change itself slightly and instead of saying, "I am dumb," it says, "You are not as smart as so and so." Or it says, "You did not finish first," etc. Even when victorious this voice lets me know I am not perfect.

Have you ever wondered why perfectionists have to be perfectionists? It's because they have the "I am dumb program" running in the background.

Blocks can be removed by eliminating the programming. The subconscious needs an enema. The junk that has built up needs to go. It needs to be replaced with more self-serving food that will assist you to be who you choose to be.

My blocks can seem huge. They may appear insurmountable. But wait! They are huge - because I am face to face with them. My nose is pressed up against the block. If I take a step back, take a deep breath, and rise above this whole block scene, I have the opportunity to see the message. Blocks are but messengers, clues to where I fail to believe in my own greatness. I don't kill the messenger. I remove the block. I can reprogram my mind so this block is no longer a block. I can believe in who I am and own my personal power. The block created by me (unknowingly) is now up to me to remove.

Insight #32

A SPARK

*To have no hope. To have no life. To have no joy. To have no love, leaves one dead. Dead is no feeling. Nothing. It is where no-thing is created. It is not an open space. It is a sealed tomb. It is where there is no spark. This no-thing need not be so. Re-choose. A desire to be and to see the spark is enough to ignite you. Often, the spark of another - sparks another. Can you spark another? Sparking another begins by accessing what brings **you** joy. By being playful. By being happy. By being this - you spark another.*

There are two kinds of nothing. One is a place where I sit quietly and let go, to receive. This is a place where outside influences take a back seat and I begin to listen to the small voice within. I hear my inner voice more easily without all the background distractions. The messages come from nothing - the place where my thoughts and body are quiet. It is where I create a space for the positive and my intuition.

The other type of nothing is what I wish to write about here. It is the nothing where I feel I have become a void. It is the nothing where I shut people out, shut love out, shut feelings out, and give up. The rock group Pink Floyd sings it best with the line in their song, "I have become comfortably numb". Unlike the space where creative thoughts flow, the dead, nothing space is not uplifting. It is a tomb. A place where the soul is locked away in darkness, slowly stagnating and being ignored until the "lack of" becomes the focus.

I have no doubt you see people like this - maybe you are like this - lacking a spark, lacking drive, passion, and vitality! Don't despair! A change is on the way.

I created the change in me the moment I chose to put the spark back into my life. All it took was one single, solitary thought. All it took was one honest heartfelt thought. I verbalized it. "I want the spark in my life. I want to feel joy! I want to feel happiness! I want to feel love." It was that simple. That request by me started a whole new energy cycle. My seed thoughts of choosing happiness, joy, and love were manifested. I reaped what I sowed and I continue to do so.

Sparking myself and keeping myself alight is not difficult. It is all contained in my thought process. It is all in my doing and my being. I am responsible and accountable for my own light. I am not responsible for another's light.

Others besides me are also looking for a spark. I, as the holder of my own happiness and love, contain the spark that can choose to kindle fires in others. I am the example. I am the leader. I, by my own choice, am a spark. This spark lights my fire and my fire sparks others to light their fire within. I become the catalyst for change. I reap what I sow. More sparks, more fires, more light, more happiness and more love. And so the energy cycle goes, getting ever stronger and stronger.

By being purposeful and joyful, I spark another, who sparks another, who sparks another, who sparks another. I am never obligated, forced, or responsible for another's light. I may only light another by being a spark. It is who I BE, that sparks the other. It is not superficial. It is not fake. It is me being genuine, that others see. It's that playfulness, that lightness that attracts their soul and offers them the opportunity to choose into their own spark.

Insight #33

PRE-DESTINY

Wanting everything mapped out for you to facilitate a smooth and safe sail just isn't so. Fear of not being right will hold you in one spot and will attract people in your life that will make you feel wrong. You know there is no right and wrong, yet the fear of being or looking wrong in the eyes of other people, to your God or even to yourself shuts everyone out. They nor you, are allowed to see your magnificence. The struggles in your life are about you standing up and pronouncing whom you are. Show your gifts, your talents. Start somewhere. Show others who you are.

One day while pondering God and the Universe I got to thinking if God wanted me to be perfect and if God wanted me to honor Him, why the heck doesn't he spell it out in plain English instead of watching me flounder around like a fish out of water? If only God would tell me what to do, I would be more than willing to do "His will." I admit I have wasted too much time doing very little of God's will. I have been waiting for the Almighty to blind me with a white light. I wanted Him to speak to me in a thunderous voice while I, the lowly subject, tremble at the whole scene.

Somehow, that has not happened.

I believe I have a purpose, but what it **is** I have no idea. I know I like helping people. I know I like making people happy. I know I like writing. Surely, this is not everything. I must be missing something. While I ponder all this, life continues. Thus, I resort to my occupation to handle everyday life, never really feeling I am doing His will.

If only I had a crystal ball that would allow me to see my way, it would be easy to know which path to take.

If I knew I could not fail before I started to do something, would I do it? Yes, of course I would. If this is true, the only thing holding me back is fear of not succeeding, fear of failure. The - "What if?"

When I was a child in school, I didn't answer the math question because I was afraid of giving the wrong answer. Being wrong would surely bring ridicule, punishment, embarrassment, feelings of inadequacy and so on. Fear of being wrong or of being a failure prevents others from seeing how magnificent I really am. I deny people my Godliness. I deny myself my own God.

Scientists do not quit after finishing their first experiment. They continue to experiment until they have just the right pieces, the right ingredients to prove their hypothesis. I must continue to experiment. I must not think of myself as a failure, but rather know each time I take action I have completed one more piece of the puzzle. I have gained invaluable experience. When the puzzle is completed, I will have in front of me the necessary ingredients and experiences to be whomever I choose to be. I will have mastered my path.

The key to this whole Insight is for me to move, to take action. I am to make a choice and move. I am to let go of the fear of being wrong and know whatever direction I take is the right direction. Think of a circle. It does not matter where I am. As long as I keep moving, I complete it.

At birth we received a great gift. The gift was free will. It is through this gift we receive freedom of choice combined with journey experiences that keep the energy cycle of creativity and manifestation in motion.

So let's all choose a path, take a step, and climb on that circle.

Insight #34

FEAR

Fear. The biggest stopper. Fear causes you to be what you are not. The fear in you is real as far as you create it and your Mind is the builder. Creating from fear and creating from love are one and the same, yet the manifestations of these choices are quite different. Create from fear. Destruction, turmoil, and chaos will manifest. Create from love. Love, harmony, and joy will manifest. Ask yourself if what you are asking to create is fear based or love based?

I am certainly not the first to write on the topic of fear vs. love. I do find the concept rather exciting. Our minds are such good creators. It is like a little energy pod sending out signals. If fear is the signal I send out, I attract all kinds of excitement that will create the very situation I was trying to avoid. We get to face our fears.

I get to face my fears. Not because God hates us and is tormenting us (although sometimes I have thought he has it in for me), but because God wants us to lose those fears. Fear is unnecessary.

Can a 100% loving person be of fear? I think not. If God wants us to be 100% loving, fear must be gone. Numerous opportunities are placed in front of us to show us we have what we have manifested, which is created from our own fears.

I remember contemplating more than once that one day, my family would all be gone. Although it was not a life threatening type of fear, it was a fear nonetheless - a fear of loss. I imagined life without my wife or children and found it a very lonely and painful place. One day my wife and

I separated and I learned firsthand what I had feared was happening. At first, my fear was incredible. I masked my fear with anger and bravado, but inside I was afraid of being alone and not being good enough. I faced those fears and survived. I sought out people who supported who I was. They supported me long enough until I could walk on my own. No longer was there fear. Eventually, I felt a transformation. The fear of loss that tore at my soul was now gone. To be true, it was so gone I wondered why I had given it any time or any energy at all. I create my own nightmares and it is only I, who has the power to remove those fears.

The only way to remove fear is to love it to death.
Fear has to be replaced with love.

Let's say I am going to create a new loving relationship (ideally) with a life partner. If I enter the relationship fearing my partner is going to be an alcoholic or will soon be cheating on me, or will spend all my hard-earned money that is exactly what will happen. The fears present in me will manifest themselves in the relationship. Whatever I wish to avoid and am fearful of, will surely show itself somewhere along the line.

I choose to let fear go and let love in. I can acknowledge fear but not be prisoner to it. Fear does not have to be the dominating force. In the example above, I can choose to enter the relationship creatively by seeing my partner as a loving person who makes choices that support our relationship. I see the best in that person and focus upon those qualities. For example, if alcohol does present itself, it is not feared. It will be handled in a loving manner. I am ever mindful I have a choice to either choose fear or choose love.

Before I begin any project, any task, any relationships, I ask myself, "Am I creating this out of fear or out of Love?"

The purpose behind my choice has a huge impact on the results I seek.

Insight # 35

FIXING OTHERS

*It is none of your business. It is not your responsibility to "fix" others, even if they come to you to be "fixed." Your only course of action is to show them who you are. Give yourself permission to show others how you express love, joy, and happiness. **Be an example.** Let others have their own experiences and their own lessons. For you to attempt to "fix" others can only come from control and manipulation. Let others choose their own experiences.*

Fixing others is an interesting concept. To be honest, I am quite sure I know what is right for others. I also suspect you would know what is right for others. If someone came to you with a problem, you would be able to tell him or her the right thing to do. I know I can do this quite easily.

Everyone is great at giving another advice. We all know how to fix the other person's problems. Papers have advice columns where people give advice about what the right thing is for others to do. TV shows have high-energy personalities who are happy to tell us what is right for us.

We are more than willing to project onto another person what we believe is the right action or direction that person should take. Someone comes to us with a problem and we, in our wealth of experiences, are more than willing to tell that person what their correct solution is.

This Insight has more to do with people who come with problems of an emotional nature or who require an answer based on one's value system. This Insight suggests it is none of my business to find solutions for people. Now it seemed a bit odd to me, I who was doing his best to be of service to his fellow man to receive an Insight suggesting my putting people on the right path (the path I think they should be on) was none of my business. It appeared my choice of helping people was being chastised. This Insight is not about ignoring, or not helping a person who comes to me for assistance, but rather to say I can only assist them by showing them who I am. Telling them to go this way or that way, to do this - to do that, or to make any choice for them whatsoever is not the correct way.

Being a person of light and love will show them the way (let's hope I have some light and love in me when they show up for help). This means **not** telling the other person what to do. Telling them the "correct" way will not teach them, for they will just be following my value system, my experiences. They must find their own answers.

The answer to people's problems is for them to find their own solutions. This is where they gain their power. Their answers and solutions may look much different from the answers and solutions I would have offered. Forcing my way or opinion upon another and appearing to know what is right for them, can only come from a place of control and manipulation. God has given each individual the freedom to choose. It is not wise or appropriate that I attempt to take that away from another person.

My role in fixing others is only to be an example of love and light; to facilitate another's growth by being an example that they may arrive at their own decisions and their own conclusions. This empowers them to make their own choices.

I may and do spend countless hours listening to the problems of others. I ask many questions of an individual who has come to me. By asking questions, they are often able to find their own answers. I still find it hard to resist, and at times fail miserably, telling people the right path to take; however, this Insight has taught me to stand back and let people own their power.

Insight # 36

SAY THANK YOU

Saying thank you for something you have received, no matter how small, allows a flow to continue. If you cannot acknowledge the small gifts you receive, you will not receive larger gifts. The Universe hears your thank you. Thank yourself, too. Say thank you to yourself when you do something well. Say thank you when you have a realization. Say thank you when the idea light bulb goes off in your head. Say thank you for your life. Allow others to give to you. Say thank you. Give to others. Allow them the chance to say thank you.

I know I am constantly receiving. I receive friendship. I receive love. I receive money. I receive opportunities. I receive experiences. I receive gifts. While I receive all these things, I am not always thankful. Yes, I am glad they came to me but I am not always thankful or as appreciative as I could be. I more or less take many of these things for granted. I only seem to acknowledge a huge receiving. I only notice and say thank you when what is received is unusually large. I deal with money every day and seldom do I say thank-you. Money I receive is allocated for various expenditures, all are deemed important – food, clothing, shelter, play, etc. I seldom stop to thank myself, the Universe, or anyone else for assisting me in creating this wealth.

Have you ever given something to someone and when they received it, they were extremely thankful? I have a daughter who is always very thankful for whatever she receives. She makes sure she acknowledges the giver and has a way of making the giver feel very special. She is constantly receiving gifts from others and I believe it is because she is open to receiving, and thankful she is receiving. She receives more and more because she is thankful.

If I give an ice cream cone to a child and they complain they only got one, I would not want to run out and buy them another ice cream cone. If I give a child one ice cream cone and they are very thankful for it, I would not **hesitate** (at some time) to give them another ice cream cone or some other gift. It is nice when I give to others and they appreciate my effort in giving. I too must learn to be thankful for what I receive.

When I receive gifts in my daily life and I am not appreciative of them, there is no open channel for me to receive more. As the child who complained about the shortage of ice cream cones, I block the gifts of the Universe by complaining I do not have enough. When I learn to say thank you for what I am given, no matter how small it appears, I open the door to receiving more.

Saying thank you is part of receiving. Most people who win the BIG lottery have no problem saying thank you. When I win a small prize in the lottery, I do not get all angry and curse that I was just a few numbers off from winning millions, I say, "Thank you universe for this small prize."

There are many things I can be thankful for: someone paying me a compliment, finding an item on sale, money flowing in, the grocery store for having my food, the gas station for having my gas, and the post office for mailing my letter. Also, when my significant other (love that term) does something special for me, does a small chore, when my children give me something, when I receive a phone call from a friend or when my monthly bills come in. Why say thank you to a bill? Because someone provided a service or gave a product to me and they trusted me to pay for it. They loaned me something, trusting I would repay it. I say thank you for the service and for the people trusting me to pay the bill. I thank myself when I pay the bill because I honor the agreement.

It is the attitude of being thankful and saying thank you for what I have been given that leads to the possibilities of being given even more. Giving to others allows them the opportunity to say thank you and increase their abundance too. Be sure you give others this opportunity. I find it fun to give to others.

Insight # 37

OTHERS

So you get to say how others should look? Be? This is not to be so. Let go of expectations of others. It is not your job to "fix" others even when you know that's why they came to you. Let others have their own experience. Let them choose how to answer their own questions. You best serve others by being an example of love. Give yourself permission to be expressive in showing the love and joy that lives within you.

My perception of life and how life should and does appear to me, often has me believing others should be in line with the way I live and conduct myself. I believe others should play by my rules and accept the same rules as I do. I come to expect others to behave in a certain manner, which is usually the way I want them to behave.

I can spend an extraordinary amount of time trying to manipulate others into doing what I believe they should do. This is a tremendous waste of energy. Not only does it pull me off my path, but it also comes from a place of needing to be in control. It is easy for me to see what is wrong with other people and not so easy to see what is wrong in me.

Sometimes people come to me asking to or expecting to be fixed. I may think this is not control or manipulation if I set about to fix them. It is. People who say they need fixing must find their own power and path. They do not need to be fixed. I can choose to allow them to have their own life experiences. Other people's experiences may look far different from my life experiences. I allow others the freedom to find their own direction, their own calling, and their own life purpose.

This may sound like I cannot help another and to some degree this is true. If I really want to assist someone along his or her path, the best way is to 'BE' an example of Love. That means to be a shining light, not by fixing others but by living my life's purpose. I express my spirit and allow others to see the beauty and joy I create all around me. When I bring light, joy, peace, and wisdom upon myself, those I meet have access to my higher energies. Through being the loving me, others will choose to be part of my energy field, not through manipulation and control, but by their own conscious choice.

Insight #38

HIDING

Be not afraid to show your love. It shall set you free. Give freely of your love, without restrictions. Show Your Love Speak your Love You are a loving person, but who can tell? The love is all bottled up inside afraid to come out. Stand tall in your truths. Stay true to your truths.

This Insight is certainly personal but, I thought there must be many others like myself who have plenty of love to show or give but don't. I give my love to a select few and that's as far as it goes. The love I have stays within me and is not expressed. There is a hesitation of showing myself as a loving person. If I show love, will people think I have gone loony? Will they push me away? Maybe they will be attracted to me and smother me.

It's interesting how society quickly embraces fear and attaches itself to it, but not to love. An example would be movies. I wonder, if we advertised a movie as a warm, loving tale leaving you tingly all over, how that would compare in sales to say a gory, destructive, evil movie? My guess is the gory one would win.

Since this Insight, I have reached out to others, but I do not feel as though I have reached out 100%, maybe about 20%. Oddly enough though, when I do reach out, speak my truth, and share who I am and what truth I have, people are mesmerized. I find they want to hear more. It's as though people want to believe, they want to know love is possible. People are desperate to hear a message of love. They want to know this life on earth has meaning – that they have meaning and a purpose. They want to grow, to understand, and move forward. When I do speak, I feel alive. I feel as though I am contributing and making a difference.

If this Insight speaks to you, come out of hiding and let yourself shine. There are people waiting for you. They need you. They want you. In fact, if truth were told, many people are spiritually hungry, but there is no one there to offer them anything to eat. Are you the one to feed them?

Insight #39
COMMITMENT

Look at your commitments. When you say you are committed to creating something or receiving something are you committed to having this or are your commitments "wishful thinking"? Do you hold the attitude of "wouldn't that be nice"? Understand you create whatever you have had, what you have now, and what you will have in the future. To receive you must first create. What will you give of your energies to create something? After creating or giving your energies, you must be willing to receive without judgment or expectation of how it (the manifestation of your creating) shows up.

I have an attitude of wishing for, instead of committing myself to what I want. Commitment is a verb. It is an action word. A word that insists I take action to manifest what I want. If there is no commitment, there is no manifestation. Some "wants" require more commitment than others do. Some "wants" require more energy.

If I take stock of where I am right now I know what I have, is exactly what I have been or am committed to. (Read that sentence again.)

To receive I must first expend the energy to create it. I must put something into it. There must be an energy transfer. If no energy transfer were required, we would have everything, wouldn't we? All things would be attracted to us.

Sitting all day visualizing is not commitment. I have been there, tried that. Visualizing surely makes for clarity, and could be a first step in commitment. Commitment is an action word and requires action. What tangible physical energies will I expend to make my creation manifest?

If it's a certain type of relationship I am seeking, I must take the necessary steps. This could look like taking out ads in the paper, or going to social meetings, joining a group, whatever it takes for me to be ACTIVE in staying committed to my creation.

If it is a material item, like a new car I must be ACTIVE in searching out the possibilities, bank loans, seeing how much is in my savings account, going to dealers, meeting salesmen, reading newspaper ads, etc.

What I have right now in my life is based upon my level of commitment. If I want to change how my future looks, I have to commit to it now. I also have to be open to receiving what I am committed to. My mind can easily see or appreciate what I say I am committed to; however, I also have to be prepared and open to receiving what I am committed to. I have to let go of the way I think it will show up. If I am so fixated on the way anything will manifest I run the risk, the possibility of missing other opportunities or ways it can manifest.

Insight #40

QUIET SPACE NEEDED

Your body is weak. Can you admit this? Is being sick a sign of weakness? Are you not allowed to be sick for fear you will appear weak and wimpy to yourself and those around you? Your body is sending you a message.Quiet time is needed. No noise, no chaos.Space is needed for energies to heal.Relax and rest. Heed this warning!

I do not like to admit to ever being sick. Sickness to me means I have lost the battle. I expect my body to run like a machine and never break down no matter how hard I push it, or how poorly I nourish it. My body is supposed to continue on, at whatever pace I set no matter what. To become sick annoys me. Sickness is a sign of weakness.

This Insight suggests sickness is the body's way of saying "SLOW DOWN."

In the fast-paced world where I choose to live, I do not take time just to stop. I have so many attention seeking devices, television, stereo, computer, car, spouse, children, meetings, sports, and other hobbies I do not take time to be quiet and relax.

I seldom allow myself to recharge fully. Sometimes I allow myself a quick charge, but never a slow full charge. If I were a battery, I would be operating at 50% charge all the time and I would constantly need quick charges to keep going. I would never be fully charged.

There must be a way I can just stop everything and create a quiet peaceful space. Is there a place where my batteries can be recharged? This place is one of rest and relaxation. It is required I make time for self so my physical body and the mental and emotional parts can be recharged for full use.

While I don't live in the same chaos and busyness I used to, I still find it hard just to stop and relax. I would much rather be doing. But, I learned it is necessary to slow down and sometimes just stop altogether. The hardest part of stopping is giving myself permission to stop. I have 1001 reasons why it is better not to stop, but in truth stopping for a while and having a full recharge makes me much more efficient and joyful when I choose to be involved in my busy life's activities. When I get sick, it is my body's way of telling me to take a rest. Perhaps if I am clever enough I can slow down, relax and recharge before my sickness tells me I have to.

Insight #41

TIME TO DO

Are you waiting for the Universe to set everything up so easy and perfect you won't need to acknowledge your own greatness? You get to make choices, have experiences and gain wisdom and understanding. **You have total free choice.** *Time to take a stand, make a choice, and do it.*

I find myself waiting for the Universe to set everything up for me. I want it all mapped out. I want to finish my life saying, "That was easy." I want all good things to fall into my lap. I don't want to toil and struggle on some difficult path to enlightenment.

This Insight declares I get to have experiences and gain wisdom. My choices, my decisions are how I gain my greatness. It is my choice what I place on my path. The Universe or God does not decide what my life is to be. That's my choice. I get to make the choices, the decisions, take the steps and actions to bring my life to a place where I want it.

I imagine telling my 10-year-old child I am sending him on a journey. I tell him where he is going. I tell him how to get there and I will guide him all the way. Where is the child's power in this? He has no choice where he is going. He has no choice on the direction he can take. He may have gained some wisdom along the way.

Now, what if the child was told he could go anywhere he wanted, I would guide him only when he asks, and I suggest to him a certain destination would be a wise choice if he so desires. Now the child has all the power, all the choices, all the learning experiences and when he reaches his destination, he will surely be the one with the power.

I no longer wait for the force, some higher self, some higher state of being, the cosmos, a spiritual awakening, to give me the blueprint of what my life is all about. It will not come. It will only come from within me. I decide what my life is about; I have total free will. I have total free choice.

When I do find myself waiting for divine inspiration I start doing what I know in my heart to do. I don't wait for the roadmap. I am going to make my own.

Insight #42

NEEDY

Accept the tools; people come into your life to assist you. You cannot do it all by yourself. Feeling upset because you require another's assistance is similar to a hockey player being upset because he needs a stick to score a goal. Let go of the "I don't want to appear needy" attitude and thank those who are in your life for being with and assisting you.

This is a simple Insight for people like myself who try to do it all by themselves. Believing I am totally independent of others is quite foolish. I am part of an inter-dependant society, an inter-dependant world. I rely on others for the clothes I put on my body, the food I eat, the house in which I live and the cars I drive. Someone once stated to me that he did not have all these "things." So, I asked if they made their own clothes. Thinking they had one up on me, they said, "Yes." I asked if they made the raw materials needed to make the clothes they wore. "No," they responded. They stated they had to rely on someone else for that. Most people probably do not grow all their own food. Did you make the house you live in? If you did, what raw materials did you use? Did you make the tools you used for building the house? Did you also start with raw materials to make your tools? You get the idea, right?

We are all dependant on others to create the things in life we want. I can manifest a television set, but I cannot create the television set. I do not have the knowledge to understand circuit boards and electronics. Nor do I choose to.

If we were an ancient tribe, each of us would have a responsibility or calling within the community. One of us would be a healer, trained in the ways of ancient herbal remedies. One would be a hunter. One would be a runner and so on. Each individual would receive assistance from the "expert" in the group when they needed it. A sick person would go to the healer. The hungry person would go to the hunter and so on. In this simple analogy do you think any one person could do it all themselves and survive? Could they be healer, hunter, and runner? I doubt it. There would be times when they need another's expertise, guidance, and experience. This is not being needy; this is being resourceful and interdependent.

When I try to do everything myself, I end up feeling quite inadequate. I attempt to conquer and master all. I believe I do not need anyone. I believe I can do it all myself. I believe I am independent. (See first paragraph if you still believe I am totally independent).

People and things are tools for me to learn and grow. I am surrounded by people; each of them possessing special skills and talents. Often, I don't take advantage of people who have talents and skills that could help me. Instead, I struggle with feelings of inadequacy while attempting to do everything solo.

A hockey player who uses a stick is far more productive than one who doesn't. The player does not feel needy when using his stick or toward the people who made his stick. It is necessary for his success.

There are people and things all around me that will propel me towards my successes. I can choose to let go and embrace the skills and gifts of others in my tribe. When I do this, I honor their being; I help them create their success, as well as my own. I allow others to be part of my success. I allow others into my life that they may encourage me to move forward. This is not being needy. This is honoring others and honoring me.

Insight #43

CHOOSE INTO YOUR LIFE

Choose into your life. Choose your life. No need to choose into anyone else's life. Choose your life. If you would but choose into your life, everything else would fall into place. It is that simple. It is simple.

It is easy for me to be caught up in the activities of other peoples' lives. This includes family, friends, relatives, and the crabby neighbor down the street. Why is it I entangle myself with the dramas of other lives? Is it love or is it drama? Am I attracted to the excitement or am I there to serve?

Imagine a theatre play. You are cast as one of the players. You have your part. You must present yourself at the right time and exit at the right time. You do your bit and your bit is part of the whole play.

Now imagine half way through the play you decide you want to be part of another scene, a scene in which you were not cast. Confusion and mayhem may take place. Now, imagine everyone decides they too want to be part of other players' scenes and parts. What confusion!

I am better off focusing my energies on my part of the play, my calling in life, choosing my own destiny rather than being sidetracked by placing myself in other people's scenes (dramas).

When I choose to follow my spirit and calling, my life falls into place. My financial situation betters, tensions lessen. More people willingly assist me and the world looks brighter. So, I choose what play I want to be in. I choose my part and am who I want to BE.

I choose into my life.

Insight #44

SEEING BEAUTY

You do not believe those who speak about your beauty and your light because you do not see these qualities in others. Begin to see the beauty and wonder in each person. Know all people are from God. Some of them wear interesting disguises. So do you.

The world can be a beautiful place. The world can be an ugly place. It is my choice and perception how I see the world. If I focus on negativity and more base energies, I will see the world as an ugly place. When I do not see a certain quality in others it is because I do not perceive that quality in me.

I can focus my energies on seeing beauty in all things no matter how ugly they may appear to me. If I can see the beauty in a person, no matter how unattractive they appear, my world will be more beautiful.

When I receive a compliment and have trouble accepting this compliment, it is often because I do not "see" these qualities in others. My focus is somewhere else, but it is definitely not on how absolutely wonderful and magnificent other people are.

I can consciously begin seeing other people for more than their outward appearance. Each person has had a fascinating life filled with fascinating stories. Everyone has suffered pain. I can begin to see how beautiful these creatures of survival really are. They really are amazing. Look and see if you can - the gifts, talents, skills every person possesses.

We are all created equal. It is my choice what I do with my life. I choose a very interesting disguise so others will not see my greatness. Most people have an interesting disguise so others cannot see their greatness. Anger, violence, prejudice, hate are all disguises. Be not fooled. It is only a disguise for a potentially perfect soul.

How do you wear your disguise?

Insight #45
INNER STRUGGLE

Your restlessness is a result of the influences moving in, around and through you. There is an inner struggle between the ego and the higher self. Know this is part of your transformation. Stop fighting. **Let love in.**

In my experience, when one is searching or trying to connect to a higher power, a higher knowing, there is an internal struggle. Like the child letting go of the parent's hand or the bird taking its first flight, so it is for those on the spiritual path. I have inner conflict when I begin to let go of my need to control, start to change my ways, make new choices, and own my power.

The ego, that part of me, which attempts to dominate, control and keep me safe... does not appreciate letting go, the risk, the possibility another source of energy is far greater than itself (Please, don't mix up ego with evil or negative influence). The ego is there to protect me, only ego has no vision. Its only function is to keep me alive.

The ego does not want me to let go or see life in a new and loving way. My ego has seen how love can and does hurt. My ego does not feel safe when I open up and become vulnerable. My ego does everything in its power to keep me feeling safe. It shows me how stupid I am. It reminds me of past failures. It creates dramas to prove itself right, over and over again. The ego is just part of me that I let control me for far too long.

I create a struggle of wills when I tell my ego what I really want is love, joy and peace, harmony and happiness in all I am and do. To prove my point I observed myself listening to a motivational speaker. After the speaker finished I felt energized, excited, and motivated to create. It did not take long for the old ego to step in and say, "Are you crazy? This will never work!" Yet, I gave it a shot. When the first block arrives and gets in my way, I call it quits and my ego says, "I told you so." End of story. Ego wins.

This Insight about struggle, tells me when I choose a new path or a new journey I can choose out of the ego survival mode. When I choose to Love, I will feel turmoil or struggle. For me, I knew this when I became restless, edgy, and uptight. I knew I was fighting a battle of ego vs. higher power. I felt more at peace when I understood this was just part of the process of letting go, the transformation to becoming more in tune with the higher. I focused on what I truly wanted and let the ego do its whimpering and whining without paying much attention to it.

Ego is always with me, protecting me. So is the higher power. Whom I choose to serve and have protecting me is my choice.

Insight #46

FEAR OF LOSS

No one ever leaves. They just move. When you travel from point A to point B, does point A leave or do you move? So it is in relationships too. Clinging to someone in a state of emotional desperation comes from a place of fear - fear of loss. This creates just that for you - a loss with much emotional discord. Allow people to be with you and you with them. When you see someone choosing out of or away from your path, let him or her go with your blessings and your love. To do so creates more love and freedom in all your relationships.

This Insight in particular relates to my loving relationships (as in life partners) and the feelings of loss that can arise when a partner chooses a different path. Fear of loss creates the same. Fear of loss creates the loss. The Universe must think of me as silly, half-brained, dimwitted, carrying around so much fear of losing something. On this temporal plane, everything is temporary. Even I am temporary, living but for a millisecond in relation to the age of the Universe.

I join a partner and we care about each other. We promise this and that (sometimes unspoken) to each other. We swear we will love each other unconditionally. When unconditionally really means as long as the other partner is following a conscious or subconscious set of rules both parties have agreed upon. "I will love you unconditionally except ..."

Both partners feel secure in this entangled life partnership and this false security works well until one partner decides to break or change the rules. Panic ensues in the partner who does not want the change. This partner fears he/she will lose something. This partner does not see it as growth. He or she sees it as threatening their comfortable relationship. When one partner chooses out of the relationship, it can become quite emotionally catastrophic for the one being left.

I find myself clinging to people who are ready to move in a different direction. There is only one reason why I would cling. That reason is I see something in or want something from the person who is leaving and I don't believe I can create this for myself. It's not because I truly love the person. It's because I don't love myself enough.

Think about it. How many of you are holding on to your kindergarten friends? Why not? Because they have nothing to offer you. It was a done deal. It was time to move on.

I can best conquer the fear of loss by thinking of myself as a whole person, not half a person who needs another half to make a whole. If I take the attitude, "I am a whole person," the need for another diminishes. This does not mean I should be forever single and unattached. It does mean though, if the relationship I am in changes, I can go with the flow knowing who I am within me, is just fine. The more I love myself, the less NEED I have to cling to another. Instead of NEED, I can replace the word NEED with CHOOSE. I CHOOSE you as my partner, rather than I NEED you as my partner. Choice is powerful. Need is not.

If I fear loneliness - I will face it

If I fear my spouse is having an affair - I will face it If

I fear I will lose a person because... - I will

It's not the Universe playing a cruel joke on me. It's fear of loss, whatever I fear, is created by me and thus manifested for me. I create the loss. I put energy into it.

I can create a new relationship, with either the same partner or a new one. I dwell not on the loss but rather the joy of creating a new and exciting relationship where I can present my gifts to another and them to me. I do this not out of need but from the joy of sharing who I am and receiving them for who they are.

To summarize: Fear of loss in my relationships is about believing I do not have the ability to create enough love in myself.

Insight #47

CONTROL

To say you are in control is similar to a fish swimming upstream and proclaiming it is in control of the river. To control leaves no room for assistance. To desire, and to create control is about fear of loss. What will you lose if you give up control? What do you fear will happen? Trust your path; the one you have chosen is all you will ever need. Being on purpose is all you do. **Let go of control.** *It's easier to go with the flow downstream. Downstream leads to the ocean.*

Control is a huge topic, which I could write about for hours. I will attempt to be brief and to the point. I will give examples of what control looks like. I will ask you to look at your life and decide if you control others or allow others to control you.

Control, or the perception of it, is one of the bigger issues I am up against. Control is when I try to force movement from a space other than love. There are people who attempt to control me and there are times I attempt to control others. There are people who allow others to control them, and there are times I allow myself to be controlled. Any one of these four control dramas result in some sort of struggle.

Control is a competition for energy. It can be subtle. It can be blatant.

If I tell someone they have to act a certain way, live a certain way, eat certain foods, dress a certain way, make love a certain way, earn money a certain way, behave in a certain way, I am using control on that person. Attempting to control leaves no room for choice. Usually, "I know better, I have experience and I am right" statements appear to justify control. What is actually happening is as the controller, I am using my past experiences and beliefs of what truth is, to decide what truth is right for another.

Ever wonder why there are power struggles? Each of us believes we possess the truth. Each one of us believes our life experiences and decisions we have made based on them (be they right or wrong) are truth. We attempt to insist that this truth, my truth is the correct truth for all.

The only time I can be in control is when I have taken time to discover and choose into my life's purpose and begin to move toward it with an open mind. The less I try to manipulate, the faster positive manifestations happen. This is because when I let go of control and the perceptions of my truths, which are generally limiting beliefs, I am free to grow. The key is to hold the focus of where I want to go.

My only focus is to be in control of my life's purpose, my life's dream. That is it.

I will share with you an experience in letting go of control.

I was among a group of five people who wanted to purchase a building for a business we were starting. To our surprise, the asking price for the building was almost double what we had intended to pay.

We started the control game with the owners of the building. They had a point of view. We had a point of view. We presented our case that this building was very overpriced. They disagreed. I could feel myself getting hot under the collar at the company preventing us from completing our purchase. I begin to align more people, more papers, more "I'm rights" on my side because I know I am right! (Can you see how the power struggle happens?) On and on it went. Then, I stepped back and I asked myself if this was the only building in town available for us to purchase. Well, of course it wasn't. I proceeded to look at many other buildings. Nothing caught my attention or excited me like the first building. The more I fought, the farther the purchase of the first building was becoming from reality.

Finally, I started to clue in to what I was doing. I asked those who were working with me to choose to let go of the control game. Our group of five just plain chose not to use this approach any longer as it was getting us nowhere. We decided to put all our energies elsewhere. We suffered some fear of loss that someone else might scoop up the building we liked so well. We let that thought go, too. We took the "We have done everything we can think of to secure this building. We keep meeting roadblocks to acquire the building, so we will back off" approach.

Weeks went by and we still had no building. We did not have the one we wanted or any other one, for that matter. Then, after waking in the middle of the night, I had an idea. Why not lease the building for a year agreeing to buy it after the year ended. The rest of the group thought this was a great idea, although we had already been told under no circumstances were the owners going to lease the building. We gave my idea a try. We called the owners of the building and presented our proposal. What do you know! The idea worked. They were more than receptive to this idea. In fact, they even started helping us find a way to make it easier to acquire the building. Wow!

The whole moral of this true story is we should not get into a control battle when we hit roadblocks. Just shimmy around them or wait for the blocks to move. Do not be rigid in thinking, be fluid.

Here is another Insight on the need to control. Letting go of control does not mean I stop taking action on a thought or idea. It will do no good just to hope the Universe will make everything all right. This thinking gives away the power.

Here's my illustration on this thought: A hockey player has a job to do. His job is to help his team by scoring a goal. He must move the puck, be aware of what his mates are doing, stay on side, and watch where he is going. He cannot control the other players on his team or the other team, but he can control where he is going. He has numerous choices on what path to take to achieve his goal. He must move. He must be continually weaving, dodging, circling, and finally shooting, to achieve his goal. He adjusts to the situation. If he just skated straight, he would encounter roadblocks and never reach his goal.

The hockey player is focused and aware of what is going on around him at all times. He can see his road blocks and avoids them. His only mission is to score a goal.

If this same hockey player practiced letting go without any movement on his part he would be standing in the middle of the ice rink being bowled over countless times by other players. He would never touch the puck. He may even think being bowled over is the Universe's way of propelling him along his journey. He would not be focused nor would he have any sense of direction. He would be relying on his mates to do all the scoring. He is, in effect, useless to his team, his coach, and himself.

Being clear about sharing the unique gifts you have inside you will put you on the ice, scoring goals. To do this, you must take action. You are only in control of what actions you decide to take toward your goal. Go for it!

Insight #48

DEBTS

*Clean up all old bills. Choose to pay them by a certain date. Not as a wish, but as a **commitment.** This (bill paying) can be an example of the power you can create. Send your bills love. Feel the joy in both the people you owe, who will be receiving the money, and the joy you will have creating the money and paying the debt. Include everybody you owe. Thank them for their patience. This need not be as hard as you make it out to be. It can be fun. **What an experiment!***

I tell myself I should not write about this Insight because at this point in my life I am not a good money manager. Money has always been a problem for me. I always seem to be a day late and a dollar short. I have had highs and lows with money. In fact, because I am self employed money tends to be somewhat of a roller coaster. Some weeks I bring in thousands and other weeks I bring in zero. I do not consider myself a spender but rather I am an avoider. I am hesitant and negligent in handling money (This is not an easy thing to confess). It feels awkward letting people know money is one of my biggest hang-ups. I have taken courses on creating money and I still fall back into the same pattern. Interestingly enough, I sent my daughters to the same money courses and they are now better off than I am. My wife wisely keeps my bank accounts and hers separate so there is some sort of stability for her. Watching me manage money drives her nuts. While we don't argue over money, I understand marriage partners tend to have more spats over money than any other issue. Sex follows a close second.

My debts are self-created. I create my own debts. I create my own money reality. There is no point blaming God for my position. I once received an email from a lady who was about to have her house repossessed. In the letter, she gives God plenty of credit for allowing her to have this house. Later, in the same letter, she blames God for taking it away. Now she is angry with God for not supporting her.

I wrote her back explaining it was not God who got her the first house. It was her credit rating and her income bracket along with how she presented herself to the lender that saw fit to allow her to carry a mortgage. Now, due to her inability to create or manage money, she was accountable for the repossession. It was not God.

My bills are a sign someone has loaned me a service or an item and trusts me to pay it back. When I pay my bills, it shows I can handle my money, and I am a person to be trusted. When I am stuck on bills, I send my bills love (I curse and swear at them sometimes too). I thank the person or company that entrusted me and I become committed to repaying them.

From the time this Insight was originally received, I have worked hard at making money my friend. I don't avoid as much and I am more accountable for my choices. I don't blame God for my debts. My situation has improved, but I still have a long way to go to be more disciplined and open to receiving money.

Make this a fun thing to do. I should heed my own advice here.

Insight #49

LIFE FORCE

There is a feeling in you that the Universe is separate from you. This is not so. The Universe is you. You are your own Universe. The Universe lives inside you. You live inside you. The Universe is internal, not external. Know the vastness, the greatness, is yours to have dominion over. The Universe is not able to control you. You control the Universe. Your Universe. If you can understand being in harmony with your Universe is foremost, you will see how simple and easy it is to create miracles in your reality.

I often think of me as me, and the rest of the world over there somewhere. The Universe is certainly way up there somewhere. This Insight suggests the Universe does not live outside of me, but inside me. God the creator lives inside me. God is internal not external.

I have heard God is everywhere and this just sounds kind of corny. It reminds me of Santa Claus watching over me to see if I am naughty or nice. The thought of God living inside me, as part of me, excites me. It makes me wake up and take notice that God is close. It makes me want to understand how I can communicate with God. If he is this close, as in inside me, perhaps I must find him, for he has certainly found me.

God gave me free will and thus he does not control my every move. God living inside me is trying desperately to assist in my choices, yet God has given me control over my own destiny. If I could find a way to be in harmony with the Universe, with God, surely God must flow with and through me. That can only be a good thing. Together, God and I can create miracles - if we are connected. If I desired anything, and God approved it, it would be.

I am a piece of God! How blessed I am. How blessed you are that the God you seek is not far away. He is right there within. All you have to do is learn to communicate with him. Easier said than done for sure, but what an opportunity. My God is so close. Your God is so close. Our God is so close.

Insight #50

MONEY

Life is not about money. Let it be said that every time money shows up being a struggle for you, it is because you are not giving enough of yourself. You are not being who you said you would be. Commit to your goals, your passions, your purpose and money will not be a source of frustration. It is easy to stray off your path. Take time to sit quietly and become connected to your goal, your dream, and your vision.

I have a theory as to what the three most difficult parts of life are for most people. I call this the SMAK theory. SMAK=SEX, MONEY and KIDS. Maybe you have noticed these three areas of life represent places where the highest energies of power struggle between people are played. There is more blaming, demands and hurt as people in relationships often conflict with each other as they deal with their own beliefs about sex, money and parenting.

I know I just wrote about money and here it is back again. Obviously, I have not gotten a handle on this money thing yet. I have my personal limiting beliefs around money, but I say money is just energy. How I attract that energy and how I use that energy is up to me. The more open I am to receiving and accepting money, the more organized I am in the area of finances, the more I am in touch with how I "do" money, the more likely I will have the power to harness this energy and transform it into a desired lifestyle.

I think, "If I take the risk to discover my life purpose and start living my life by making choices of who I really want to BE, I may not make it. I may put myself in a worse financial situation." I respond, "What is the worst that can happen? Will I die?" I doubt it. The strange thing about being in survival mode is I am kind of dead. I am not living life to my fullest. It is like seeing a million dollars on a table and allowing myself to take only a one-dollar bill. My life is worth a million dollars. When will I stop picking up the lonely one-dollar bills?

When I begin to be me, and put my energies into the areas that excite me, there will be a return on my energies. This can look like money.

For example, a man works for many years as a cook in a restaurant. He is paid xxx amount of dollars. His benefits include vacation time, holiday pay, sick pay, and he receives just enough money to buy necessities with a small amount left over. If he saves hard he can, after a few years, purchase a luxury item - a new car perhaps. He is not unhappy with the work he does, although he knows there is something more to life than this. There just has to be. These thoughts happen in his 30's when life is not as great as it was going to be when he was in his early twenties. At forty, panic sets in. He thinks, "How much of my life has been wasted?"

This same man has a great singing voice. He sings to himself all the time. Sometimes at work he sings. He loves singing. However, singing will not put food on the table. Besides, he feels as though he is not good enough and so he goes on about his cooking. He secretly wishes someone would walk up to him one day and say. "Nice voice. Here's a million dollar contract to sing for us." Oh, dreams.

If he could only recognize singing is what brings him joy. If only he could recognize this, he could share that joy with others, if he would but sing. He must become aware of the gifts he has. He must follow his dream, his heart. This is where the energy comes in. By following his heart, his dream, his energy level increases too. His life is no longer centered on survival; it is centered on singing and that is real joy. As long as he can sing, he creates joy. The energy of this can only attract joyous things, joyous people and before long he will have all those things he has dreamed of.

I believe following my dream does create abundance. The amount of energy I create in living my joyous dream is reflected in the amount of abundance in my life. When I commit to living my dream, and teaching what I know, I will have the abundance I seek, both financially and spiritually.

Insight #51

ORDER

It is necessary, for you to receive abundance; your life must be put in order. There must be a structure in place for abundance to manifest. Imagine asking for a new car. What if you hadn't taken driving lessons, earned a license, become familiar with the rules of the road, and paid for insurance? For you to manifest a car without these prerequisites would not be for your higher good. It could cause harm, see? So it is, in all areas of your life. Become disciplined, organized and structured in the areas you want to receive abundance.

The Insights just keep on coming around the subject of money and abundance. It is one of my weakest areas.

This Insight suggests for me to receive abundance, I have to prepare the way. I am mistaken if I think the Universe hands out gifts to people for no reason. People who receive are people who have asked and who have an avenue that allows them to receive.

Observe the winners of the lottery. Most of the winners of the lottery do not have money issues in their life. Ever noticed? Very seldom has a lottery winner proclaimed they were destitute before they won. Recently, I watched a man and his family win mega millions. It wasn't the first time they won. This father was already a self-made millionaire from his business as a restaurant owner.

Part of the secret of receiving abundance is having order and structure. Imagine if I just won ten million dollars, but I have no bank account to deposit the money. I would have to open a bank account. If I open the bank account first with the intention of depositing ten million dollars, I have created an avenue for receiving. At this point, you may say you already have a bank account. Yes, this may be true, but did you establish a bank account with the intention of depositing ten million dollars?

Asking for what I want is only the first part of the equation to receiving. Believing I can have it is another part of receiving. Yes, believing it. Being open to receiving is the other part of the equation. The last part is preparing the way.

My 14-year-old daughter would sure like to have a car. Think of the freedom she would have. The independence! The joy! How could the Universe and her not work together to manifest this wonderful invention for her? If she was able at this time to manifest this vehicle, it could prove deadly for her or someone else. Let's say, "Poof" there is the car. She gets in with no training, experience, or knowledge of the rules of the road. She has no knowledge how to operate a vehicle, yet she drives away. The car, the freedom and the joy would soon be gone if she were to have an accident. However, if she prepares the way and learns the rules of the road, takes driving lessons, appreciates and respects her manifestation, the car will serve her well. The timing of the manifestation must be correct. We don't receive things that will cause us harm.

The car analogy works in all phases of life. "Oh, if only I had a million dollars I could manage my money." Not! If I cannot manage a little money, how will I manage an abundance of money? The problems will only increase, not decrease. When I open bank accounts, learn about taxes; understand investments and the value of real estate, depreciation, etc. it is more likely I will receive what I ask for.

"Oh, if only I had the perfect significant other, I could have a happy relationship." Not. If I cannot manage my current relationship, how will I manage the most important relationship? Relationship problems will only increase, not decrease. I could learn better communication and take personal growth courses. I could read books that teach about relationships. I could learn about the opposite sex. I could learn about sex, money, and kids and see how it all fits in to a relationship. I could learn about giving and receiving. I could learn about sharing. I could learn about the power of forgiveness. I could learn about letting go of control. Then, it is more likely I will receive the relationship I have asked for.

"Oh, if only I had the perfect job, I could earn more money." Not. If I cannot excel where I am, how will I manage the perfect job? Work related problems would only become more challenging. I could take communication courses; learn about service and what makes business tick. I could learn business practices. Then, it is more likely I will receive what I asked for.

I hope you get the picture by now. I can ask away to my heart's content, but if I have not made some order, some avenue whereby I am ready, prepared and mature enough for the inflow of abundance, it will not manifest.

I look at what I am asking for and know I must put that part of my life in order. I cannot have the BIG until I can handle the small.

Insight #52
MOVE FORWARD

To give up. To choose out. To quit. This wastes energy. It is a drain. There is more energy required to do nothing, to give up, to quit, than there is to move forward. All life moves, including yours, even when you are standing still. How fast you want to move is up to you.

There have been times I wondered if I should just quit. Others seemed to have it so easy compared to me. For what I was receiving it appeared the amount of energy I expended to create anything was far more than I reaped in reward.

I just wanted to give up. "Please someone! Make my life easy. I don't want to put up with all the crap I have to deal with. I want my life to be simple. I want security. I want peace. I want... (You fill in the blanks).

This Insight shows doing nothing, quitting, requires more energy than moving forward. Life moves. Life continues with or without me. Life just goes on. Time (and energy) stands still for no person.

It seems a bit of a slap in the face to realize the energy expended in creating what I want and moving forward to that place is simpler and easier than doing absolutely nothing. I better make a choice and move toward it. Choosing is less taxing than not doing anything.

I had better get moving.

Insight #53

LETTING GO

Letting go of the past cannot be done by holding on to the past! To let go is to let go. You cannot sell your old car and keep it too. Trust that after you have let go and created some new goals a shifting will take place. Keep your ears and eyes open for when the avenue shows up. You may take any avenue presented to you. If you do not see, or choose not to take the avenue presented, it is a missed opportunity. A missed opportunity is not bad; it simply means more time on your part is required while the arranging for the next opportunity is put in motion.

I say I have let go of my past, when in fact, all that has happened is my past has been placed into a temporary storage area in my brain. Like an old file folder stuffed into an old filing cabinet, so it is for my past experiences. The unfortunate thing about this type of letting go is the file folder can be retrieved at will and this usually happens when a similar event takes place. My brain is an idiot. It is a data bank. It collects data from which I make decisions. If it sends me the same data, I am most likely going to make the same choices.

There is no doubt my past can be a place where many cruel and hurtful events have occurred. Putting these events in the back of my mind or just letting time heal them does not suffice. I must be willing to let them go. The file folder must be destroyed. Otherwise, a true letting go has not taken place. **To let go is to let go.**

The best method I know for letting go or destroying the past is to love it to death. By embracing my past and seeing the good, no matter how small, I begin the process of destroying my past. I must love my way out of the past. Forgiveness of self and others is important. Loving self is critical.

Is it possible for me to see something good out of all the bad? Was it not the 'bad' experiences in my life that put me on the course to spiritual enlightenment? The "bad" experiences of my past were a gift.

Why let go? When I let go of my past, the hurts, the resentments, the anger, the hate, I free myself of negative energy, which hangs like a weight around my neck. Once free of this weight I feel lighter, more energetic and more in tune with who I am. No longer do I suffer from, "I don't want to face the world" syndrome, instead I cannot wait to see what good things will come my way. It is like house cleaning. If I have a closet full of junk, there is no room for new stuff. There will never be room for new stuff until I throw the old stuff out. So it is with my mind. Clean out the old stuff and make room for the new.

Part of creating new stuff is to ask for what I want, and then create new goals. What is it I want? After letting go of the past, I keep my ears and eyes open - for new opportunities will present themselves to me. I will be able to put new things in my closet. I get to choose what new things I attach to myself. If, in hindsight, I see I missed a great opportunity, I do not fret, for another opportunity will soon follow. I am patient while the energies work their way around to me again. Be ready.

Insight #54

TODAY

Live today like you are a runner on a mission. Live full of life and enthusiasm. Do not concern yourself with what is ahead. Take one step at a time and deal with any blocks as you come to them. Stay "in the moment" and create what you want in today's reality.

I want to go through life with a purpose. I will make this something I choose. I will make it something that excites me - uplifts me, energizes me. What is it that would uplift me and give my life even more meaning? What would I choose to do if I only had six months to live? Why don't I do that now? At least I should begin! I do not need to worry about what is ahead. Alas though, I stop before I even get started. My own fears and frailties supported by so many past experiences (seen as truths) cause me to lose my dream of being who I want to be.

There is no need for this. Just begin. It is that simple. I take one step and when I am ready, I will take the next step. It all sounds so easy. Yet, I am not feeling any more on purpose than I ever have. I still know I am not living my life to the best of my ability. I am not doing what truly calls me. I was once told, when I am not sure what the first step is, answering this question will help: Right now, at this time, what is it I know to do? If I listen, there is an answer to this question.

If I come up against a block in accomplishing what it is I want to do, I can change my perception and begin to call my blocks *opportunities*. I use the block as an opportunity to learn and grow.

I choose to stay in the present and live 100% today. Not tomorrow, today. In doing this, I create the type of life and experiences I want to manifest and know they will arrive.

The time is now.

Insight #55

BLOCKS

It is not possible to know what all your blocks in the future will be because you haven't created all of them yet. So, be in the moment. Be present today. Tomorrow never comes. It is already here. Blocks, or opportunities (sometimes I call them painful opportunities), are in front of me all the time. I create these blocks. I have the power to break them. It is my own limiting beliefs, my own subconscious programming, and my pre-adult decisions that create these blocks.

I know I have many blocks (opportunities), to raise myself to be the person I want to be. I also know I have conquered many blocks. As a result of conquering these blocks, I am a better man today. In personal relationships, I have overcome adversity making me much wiser and more compassionate. I have learned love cannot be controlled. It cannot be manipulated. It just is. I have learned to control my anger, realizing that acting with anger, does not promote who I want to be.

This Insight was in reference to me asking, "What blocks do I still have in front of me?" I figured if I could find this out I had an advantage. I could become conscious of the block. I could become aware of it and see it when it appeared. I would be in a better position to conquer the block more readily and speedily.

This was the theory, but as the Insight suggests, I have not created all my blocks yet. Here I was hoping they were all childhood blocks that just needed to be re-programmed or cleaned out. Instead, I receive information I may, at this very moment, be creating my next block. Dang!

This Insight suggests I be in the present. I should deal with what is at hand and not be looking to the future. Makes sense when I think about it. Concerning myself with my future, ignores my present. If I take care of, handle, deal with, grow in my present, my future can never be far away.

Insight #56

CLOSET CLEANING

Smile at yourself. There is no need for condemnation here. Have you ever cleaned out your closet? Did you notice as you begin to empty this and that from your closet you create a mess, chaos, and debris? You must rearrange and reorganize everything back into the closet. A fair amount of energy is expended to put a closet in order. So it is with you, right now. Your closet (of life) is being emptied and everything appears in a state of disarray. You are deciding what to put back in your closet and what to throw out. Let go of the old. Say thank you for when and how it served you. Once reorganized, your closet will have new space, which you may choose to fill with new and different things. What will you put in there?

There came a time when I sat back and took a hard look at my life. I began to ask myself questions like, "Who the heck am I and where did I go wrong? Why is my life not like I planned it to be?"

I talk to myself saying, "It isn't fair! I've worked hard, sacrificed plenty. Somehow, I feel as though I came up on the short end of the stick." Sometimes that looks like financial burdens, relationship chaos, or a feeling of being totally disconnected. It's as though how I thought my world should look and how my world did look (reality) somehow got mixed up. The two are not in sync. Something is missing. It is time I took a step and cleaned up some debris.

This debris is in my closet. Not the closet in my home (Ok maybe that one, too) rather, I am referring to my life closet. I may no longer have use for many things in my closet. They do not serve me anymore. These may be old beliefs, old ways of doing things, holding on to past hurts and painful experiences and so on. I ponder my life and ask myself if there are things in my closet of life that should be cleaned up.

When I peek in my closet, what is it I no longer need? Do I really need that petty bill staring at me? I know I promised to pay it a number of times. I am going to take that bill and pay it right now. I know I have withholds (unspoken communications) I want to address with certain individuals or groups. Now is the time for me to clean out this debris and handle my unspoken words. In my closet lives, "I can't and I am not good enough, I am not strong enough, I am poor, I am not worthy." All this debris lives in my closet.

As I clean up my closet of life, I notice my world seems to be in chaos (It usually is anyways, so this is just a chaos bonus). All those yucky things I have been hiding are spread out before me. It is similar to having a mini tornado ripping through my world. This is not bad. This is all part of the cleaning process. Have you ever tried to clean out a messy cupboard and not dispose of any items? It just does not work. Cleaning up your life works the same way. Yes, there will be a mess and chaos. Yes, there will be choices, choices and more choices.

I could choose to leave the mess and live in perpetual chaos (my wife says I would prefer this). Yet, like a whirlpool, perpetual chaos uses a great deal of energy going around and around, yet going nowhere. If I choose to put everything back in the closet, I am back to square one.

If I choose to let go and rid myself of some things in the closet that are no longer useful, there are more choices of what I can put back in the closet. Some things have been in the closet far too long and need to be thrown out. Forgiveness is a sure way to rid me of some of these closet fillers. I say thank you to the things I am throwing out, for in some way they have served me. I let them go.

When I let go of those useless pieces in my closet there is more room in the closet, more room for new ideas, new energies and new choices. Now I can decide what new things I want to put in my closet of life. I make choices about the things that will work for me. It could be I choose a money management program, healthier relationships, a new fitness and health program for my body or something else I desire or need.

I now have the choice of what I want to put in my closet. It is my choice.

Insight #57
EQUALITY

Know all mankind was created equal. Remember this. Do not put yourself beneath another, nor above another. No one is better or higher than another, no matter what the physical manifestations may look like.

Here is an Insight I struggled to understand. I asked myself, how is it possible all people are created equal? Physically, I can see differences. Height, weight, looks, are all different. Mentally, some people are more intelligent than others. Even spiritually, some people seem to have reached a place of peace and contentment, while others still play in the lowest places. So how is it possible we are created equal?

To answer this, I best put aside the physical body. It is obvious we are not all the same physically. I best discard the idea equality is physical. I imagine I have no physical body. No hair, no skin, no muscles, no bones. What is left? To some there is nothing. To others, me included, what is left is my soul. My soul resides in my physical being. It is from this soul I am created as an equal.

Here's an analogy that may help. Imagine a whole pie. This is the Creator. Divide the pie into four and you still have the Creator only it is split. Each piece of pie is whole on its own and it is also part of the whole pie. It is separate, yet part of the whole. At the time the pie was divided, each piece was created equal. They were all the same. Each of those pieces of pie (us) has from their own choices (free will), undergone different experiences. Some pieces of pie play in the muck and others choose to seek higher realms. While they appear worlds apart, they were still created from the same source (the whole pie). Some pieces of pie appear more spiritual, more in tune. Some don't. But these are just the manifestations of their choices. In truth, the pieces of pie are still part of that perfect whole. Each piece of pie (soul) has the same opportunity to return to the creator enhanced with the experience of freewill, choice, and faith.

It would be foolish to put myself beneath another or to think myself less than another. It would be foolish to think myself above or higher than another. All of us, **without exception**, are part of that perfect pie (I am a piece of pie). I may have made interesting choices along the way, but that can never take away my wholeness of self and my spiritual connection to the whole.

We are all equal. Another way to say this is we all have equal opportunity. No matter what environment, no matter what difficulties, no matter what life throws at me, I have and WE ALL HAVE that piece of God living in us, allowing us the power to make our own choice as to whom we will serve.

Insight #58

THE DEVIL

There is no devil, only the losing sight of the light. Show others the light by being a light.

Amazing, but true! No devil. When things are bad it's not the Devil's fault. When I do things I would consider less than Godly, it is not the Devil's fault. When tragedy strikes, it is not the Devil's fault. Nothing is the devil's fault because there is no devil. There is no force opposing God attempting to cause me pain or steal my soul.

The devil is fear based. The devil concept grew from my own animal-like fear... that someone, something, some ghost or some force was out there trying to sabotage me. This is absolutely absurd.

There may be evil, the doing of ungodly acts, but there is NO devil influencing me. There is no entity attempting to steal my soul. I find the whole concept almost laughable.

Belief in the devil is fear based, not love based. Teaching of the devil is used for no other purpose than to place fear into another. Be it said if I ever hear anyone teaching or preaching the devil, I turn and walk away - for I have just met evil.

I choose my life be focused in love. May my Light shine and may that shining light, shine on others.

Insight #59

PEOPLE

Thank all people who show up in your life. It is no accident they show up when they show up. You created them so you may move forward. You create all people who show up in your life. It is no accident they show up when they show up. You created them so you may move forward.

There are people in my life I enjoy. Other people in my life make me feel less than joyful. Which person(s) in my life bring me the least joy? I spend a moment and it's easy to think of one of these people right now?

The people in my life right now are there because I attracted them. I create people in my life so I may move forward.

If I fear flying, all kinds of people and opportunities will show up to challenge this fear. Not because the Universe is cruel and unkind, but because the Universe does everything in its power to show me fear does not belong in my life.

The Universe does everything in its power to assist me in moving forward out of fear. If I fear anything and what I fear keeps showing up, it is up to me to get in touch with that fear, to recognize it and deal with that fear. I embrace and love that fear to let go of it. When I do, a miraculous thing happens. The fear goes away. If I do not fear, it will very likely not show up again. If it does come into my life again, it will not have the same effect or power on me as when I feared it. The energy is different.

If I fear controlling people, one will enter my stage of life. I may not marry one or have an intimate relationship with one (or I may), but I will encounter them somewhere along my travels. It could be at work or while enjoying recreational activities. Whatever I fear will show up.... somewhere.... until I can face my fears and love my way out of it.

All people I am having difficulty with are there as guides to assist me in moving forward. I have attracted them, based on my own fears, to move me to a higher level. By having fear, I attract them with the Universe's assistance.

Insight #60

AN AWAKENING

There is an awakening in you. A fine-tuning of vibration communication is taking place. You are warned to slow down, to pay attention to the road ahead of you. Become aware of what opportunities come your way. While you may not see it at this time, there is a flurry of activity, preparing a way for you, an opportunity. If you miss this opportunity, another will soon follow.

I begin to realize I am part of a bigger picture. I question my existence and ponder my purpose in life. I know of religion, but I do not know of the glory proclaimed by such religions. I can imagine what glory would be like. Few have ever touched that space and been able to enlighten the rest of us as to where it is, what it is, or how it feels.

I fit in the category of not comprehending fully the state of enlightenment. Yet, I have seen glimpses of it. Glimpses so small, so fractal from what I believe to be the bigger picture. I believe most people, if they were cognizant of their environment and feelings, would touch that place of enlightenment. It is a higher place than what I know or understand to exist. I find when I have love in me, when I am in a loving space; I am more easily able to "hear" my inner God.

I attract this state of enlightenment. When I am able to quiet the chatter within me, energies awaken me to the knowledge I am not alone. I find I am not separate; I do have overseers and guidance from an invisible-to-me source. The moment I realize I am not separate from the universe I can choose to open myself to receiving higher energies, thoughts, and ideals. I am a transmitter and a receiver. I can tune myself to receive inner messages and I can (if I choose), transmit those messages in any way I wish (this book would be an example of receiving and transmitting messages).

I confirm I perceive these energies are working with me. I have a responsibility to myself and to my fellow man to discipline myself in the act of listening.

Listening is accomplished by awakening the energies. I awaken to the energies in many ways. I can listen while meditating (although I am not a big meditation fan), while driving the car (with my eyes open), or when playing loud music. There are many ways to accomplish listening. The point is to listen. Listen to what? Listen to communication from my God, my higher power - whatever name I choose to give my source. Awakening the energies takes place when listening. Listening happens when I communicate with God.

Recently, I went to a natural health practitioner who had a machine that could measure my emotional responses. The practitioner asked me why I was there and I explained it was a physical condition. I won't go into details but suffice it to say my body was not operating at 100%. I already knew the physical condition was caused by fear and worry but I did not want to admit it. I thought, "How can I possibly teach others how to remove fear and worry when I cannot do it myself?" Hence, I was at the natural health practitioner hoping she could assist me in removing my fear and worry.

My arms, legs, and head were wired to a machine that looked similar to a lie detector. It measured the electrical impulses from my body. This machine scanned my emotional body and found I had two predominant emotions. Fear and worry (no kidding I thought).

She asked me to sit quietly and visualize numerous peaceful settings. When my body reached the correct level of peace, she would inform me. So as I live close to the ocean, I visualized the sand and sea. She told me what I was thinking about caused no response in the readings. This was not working. The machines readings were not changing. I also live near a lake, so I visualized myself on a raft lying in the sun, floating on the water. That too, was not working. I began to wonder if she turned the machine off. I thought to myself, "Visualize white light." I sat in the chair and visualized white light surrounding me. Immediately she said, "Whatever you are doing you just sent the machine off its scale." I had only been visualizing white light for about 5 seconds at this point. I continued for about another minute when she asked me to stop.

Upon opening my eyes, she looked surprised and asked me what I was thinking of when the machine's readings went off the scale. I was tempted to say a Playboy Magazine, but I resisted and told her I visualized white light. She rescanned my emotions using the machine to find my fear and worry diminished 50% from the first scan. I achieved a 50% reduction in fear and worry emotions by visualizing white light for just over one minute.

So what is my white light? I have always imagined it as white light. "No kidding," you say. Whenever I visualize white light, I imagine it to be sending information, guidance, and love. I imagine I am a computer downloading some important program from a higher source.

The awakening of energies happens when I choose to receive and accept there are higher energy sources I can tap into. Awakening to energies coming to me is a choice I make. This energy is available to anyone and everyone regardless of race, creed, economic status, geographical location, environmental condition, ethnic background, or religious or non-religious upbringing.

For myself, my energies awaken through the visualization of White Light. You may choose to visualize whatever you believe will work for you. Choose something uplifting you know arrives from a higher source.

Insight #61

DAVID AND GOLIATH

To believe life has to be a struggle still lives within you. To have a life of freedom and ease is still viewed by you as impossible. You focus on overcoming adversity. David (you) against Goliath (whomever or whatever you feel, where you can be the underdog). These battles excite you. These battles make you feel alive. The surprise is there is only one David and he is you. There is only one Goliath and he is you. You create your David's. You create your Goliath's. How many times do you have to slay your Goliath's before you realize what a powerful being you are? Can you stop slaying these Goliath's and just move on? Can you kiss Goliath, hold his hand, and show him compassion? Can you love your Goliath?

Oh, how I love the excitement of a battle! Not just any battle, I crave the ones where I am the underdog, victimized and treated unfairly. I like fighting giants? Who is my Goliath? At different times, it has been the government, my parents, my religion, my insurance company, management, my spouse. I crave a battle. How exciting! When I fight, I feel alive and full of energy.

In my battles, more times than not I am victorious. While the victory is sweet, I never come away unscathed. I have emotional battle scars to prove I was at war. What I fail to realize is the victory that took place I created. I create the battles. I create the possible outcome. The struggle, which makes me feel alive and like I have a noble purpose, is a distraction for me. How many times must I prove to myself my own greatness? These battles are distractions that prevent me from being who I am. I am not my battle. I am not my struggle. I am an alive, vital, loving force that does not need to conquer self-created foes time and time again.

Being able to come from a place of compassion and love will render the positive results I seek. When I move away from areas where I find myself in a struggle, I begin to see the results I want without having to engage in a battle. I allow the outcome to be in my favor without the emotional struggle, hostilities and anger. I allow the belief - life is not about struggle. I believe whatever I want in my life I can have by accessing the power of peace, harmony, joy, and love.

It is truly amazing when I stop fighting and start creating. Life goes from stress to pleasure, from exhaustion to relaxation. Look at the battles you are involved in and decide if they are really necessary. Do they support who you are?

Insight #62

DIRT FROM THE PAST

Stop complaining about your past and move on. Dirt from the past. Your past is like a crushing weight on you. You created your past! You are still carrying this past with you! Who do you think has the power to clean you of this past? YOU DO! To become clean is about forgiving yourself. Demand a perfect reality. Create this by choosing how you want your life to look, now. Your future is now, so choose to create it, now. Keep moving forward and go for what you want. There are those who will assist you.

There can be no doubt my present reality is based upon past choices. Those decisions I made in the past take me to my current state. If I want to know my future, all I have to do is look at my past. My past will be my present and future unless I make different decisions and choices.

The past follows me wherever I go and no matter what I do. I remember a lady friend, a single parent, telling me she was going to move away from her home and take her children with her. This was not an easy task for her, as she needed Family Court approval. After a legal battle with her ex-husband, the judge ruled she could pack her bags and legally leave. She told the judge by leaving, her life would improve because she would have more of _____ and less of _____ (you fill in the blanks). She felt if she could change her environment her life would be different.

She phoned me months later from her new home, located on the opposite end of the country and somehow she managed to recreate all the same emotional problems and entanglements thousands of miles away.

I cannot run from my past. I can only let it go. The only way to let it go is to acknowledge it and forgive myself. Then I have the opportunity to re-choose. Upon re-choosing, I create a whole new reality.

I create the reality I want. Demand it! I have the power to choose it and live it with ACTION. I move towards it. It's not enough just to hope it happens. Action must be taken. The more I focus and move toward the new me, the new choice, the more likely people will show up to assist me. People or events always support me when I am moving toward a goal.

Insight #63

THE FUTURE

In every moment, there is a now. To wait to do, is to wait now. To move to do, is to do now. Everything is as it should be. What the future holds is what you create today. What you hold today, is your future. All is one and the same.

The present is the future. I conceive everything is happening at once and time movement is like a circle expanding out rather than being linear. In every moment, there is a present. There is a now. There is a present tense in every moment.

To wait to do, is to wait now. To wait also becomes present tense. Waiting for the future is pointless because there is no future. There is only now. To move to do, is to do now. Whether I am moving or waiting, I am still in the now. What I create is my choice.

The future holds what I create today. If all is in the now, my future is right now. What am I creating in my now?

Everything is as it should be. The reality I have in my now is perfect. Why? I created it. I really am master of my own destiny.

What I hold today in my now, is my future. My thoughts, beliefs, and actions now are my future manifestations. They are happening now and are as they should be (because I am the one who believes what I believe and I am the one who thinks what I think) thus, whatever I create is perfect because I am the creator.

Does all this sound like mumbo jumbo? Let me say this simpler.

There is no future. There is only present. Change your present and you change your future. I know, I know, I said there is no future. Let's say it again.

There is no future. Change your present and you change your future present.

It is now and my future is now.

Insight #64

SHINING LIGHT

Let your light shine! It takes less energy to allow your light to shine than it does to remain in darkness. Let my light shine!

I have the potential to shine in everyday life. I have the necessary resources within, to help me shine. All I have to do is make the choice whether to use those resources that will enable me to shine.

So what is shining? Well, it is not that scary movie by Stephen King. The shining I am referring to is the ability to allow myself to be a loving, caring, joyous person. When I shine, I radiate. I glow. When I shine, I am content. When I shine, I exude peace. When I shine, I show mercy. When I shine, I am a forgiving person. When I shine, I shine.

Having said that, I imagine many people will respond, "That shining thing you talk about Phil, is all fine and dandy. How can you expect me to shine when I have all these bills to pay, kids to clothe and feed, and health problems to worry about? I cannot possibly shine until I have.... (You fill in the blank)."

Shining is a state of being. It is a state of mind. It is where I choose to place myself. Shining is showing my gifts, talents, spirit, and dreams. Shining is showing who I am. Not the surface me, but the inner, God-aware part of me. It is the part of me who knows LOVE and chooses to let it through.

It takes less energy to allow my light to shine than it does to be in darkness.

What is darkness? It is not evil. It is not the devil. Darkness is the absence of light. Darkness is the absence of shining. If shining is a choice, living in darkness is also a choice. I can choose not to shine.

The act of choosing to live in darkness requires more energy than choosing to shine. You see, it requires much energy to harbor resentments, hold on to hate, be unforgiving, angry, jealous, envious, to distract myself from my calling, be unhappy, cruel, vindictive, hurtful, discontent with people, discontent with my finances, and discontent with life. This is darkness and it requires far more energy to "be" in darkness than it does to "be" in light.

I ask myself whether I live in "light" or "darkness." Which would I prefer to live in? It is my choice. I know I have lived in some dark places and I know it has not served me. I have never felt at peace when choosing to live in darkness. I and only I, have the power to make this choice - to live in the light or in the dark.

I had to hit the bottom of my barrel before I realized I had to look at and choose my priorities in life. Choosing peace, light and love as a way of being, is my key to breaking free from the darkness.

Here's an example of the power of light.

Imagine you are standing in a dark room and the door is closed. There is absolutely no light. It is pitch-black. Imagine just outside the door of this pitch-black room there is a light on. There is a 100-watt bulb about two feet from the closed door. While you are in your dark room, open the door to the light.

Observe.

When you opened the door that led to the light, did the light shine into the dark room you were in or did the darkness of the room you were in pour out into the room with the light?

The light penetrated the dark; however, the dark cannot penetrate the light. Light is always more powerful. Darkness is simply an absence of light.

For me to let my light shine, I have to turn on my inner light. I choose how I am going to BE. I choose my attitudes, emotions, path, state of mind, and my way of being.

If I want more energy, more joy, more abundance, more peace, and more love, I must let go of darkness and embrace light. I let my light shine.

Shining is a choice and we all have the ability to choose it.

Insight #65

SEXUAL ENERGY

As you become more attuned, cleaner, more pure, more on purpose with your life you experience a surge of energy. Have you chosen a sexual arena to manifest this abundance of energy? You have been taught an abundance of sexual energy is wrong or imperfect. Sexual energy is just energy, like any other energy. This is your way of expressing that abundance of energy. It is not wrong. You may consider you have numerous areas where you can express this energy in a creative manner. Sex is a good indicator of how your life force energy is, in the present. A depletion of energy will nearly always result in shutting down the sexual drive.

At one time, I went through a great period of personal growth. I was thinking new thoughts and seeing life in new ways. I had forgiven and continue to forgive people and myself. I was kinder to others and myself. I saw more beauty in other people, the environment, and myself. I let go of the negatives such as hate and anger. I began to feel healthier, freer and better about who I was. I felt connected to myself, to those around me and to God. This produced in me a somewhat natural "high." This energy was drugless for sure, yet almost as intoxicating.

The energy surging through me was absolutely wonderful. I found myself becoming more sexually alive. I began questioning whether this was acceptable.

The Insight that followed, which answered this question, explains sexual energy is just energy and while it is not wrong to manifest positive feelings in a sexual way there are other ways to express energy for creative purposes. The act of sex was neither bad nor good. It just was. I could have just as easily channeled this abundance of energy into sports, work, play, reading, writing, or any other avenue of my choice.

The last bit of information let me know desire for sex is a good indicator of my present energy level. A depleted supply of energy results in less desire. An increase in energy increases desire.

The Sexual Energy Insight suggests taking part in sex is fine, but there are also other ways, other choices I can make to acknowledge or express the heightening of or abundance of energy.

Insight #66

RULES

While rules are necessary to promote order, they need to be balanced with an equivalent amount of energy dedicated to doing nothing but having pure fun. There needs to be a balance between rules and fun! Are your rules restricting your freedom? Are your rules restricting another's freedom?

A facilitator at a conference I once attended told me, "There is freedom in rules." I was not convinced. I did not want rules in my life. I did not want to follow the same path as everyone else. I wanted to be different.

The results to this point in my life were a broken marriage, four kids to feed, and an empty bank account. I suppose this is somewhat different, but not the kind of different I was really looking for or needed. Sure, I broke rules. I broke the rule of paying for my electricity. I broke the rule of paying for my telephone. I broke the rules of eating healthy. I broke the rules of paying my share of taxes. I broke many rules. Breaking rules did not allow me freedom; rather it constricted me and held me back. I learned the electric, telephone and tax people had their own set of rules. I learned about collection agencies and their rules. The rules I kept breaking were causing me more stress in life than I ever dreamed.

Rules keep a sense of order and balance. I am one who never cared about keeping financial records or even reconciling my checking account. I can honestly tell you keeping financial records and reconciling bank accounts is far easier than not doing it. Gone are the days (mostly), when I write a check and guess, sometimes even correctly, at how much is in the account. Gone are the stressful days of NSF (not sufficient funds) checks because I was too lazy and too non-conformist.

Today, I know exactly what I have in the bank and exactly how much is budgeted for living expenses, etc. There is freedom in following the rules.

Some rules are rules that make no logical sense. They are inherited or learned. Recently, my mother confessed when I was a child no matter how tired, clean, or sick I was, she insisted on giving me a bath every night. She recalled stories of carrying me in from the car whilst I was fast asleep and plopping me straight into the tub. Why? It was just a rule, a habit. One that did not make a whole lot of common sense, nor did it show much compassion for tiny, cute, little me.

Many rules are about control. "There will be no playing until all the work is done." Now, what kind of rule is this? This is a rule that says "work first play later." What harm is there to turn it around the other way? Play first, work later. "Oh," says the skeptic, "but the work won't get done." That, my friend, is just a story, a fallacy. If you ask properly and leave no doubt the work must be done, it will be done.

Many rules restrict my own enjoyment of life as well as others. Have you ever been with a person who is so bent on adhering to the rules they take the fun right out of the game or the project? I think of a sports coach who drives the game rules into the children's heads forgetting it can and should be fun for them. They need to learn the rules, but there also needs to be fun in learning. There needs to be a balance between having fun and having rules. Both are possible.

The rules I create give me a sense of order from which I can choose to move forward toward the playfulness required by the child within.

Rules balanced with fun equal's freedom.

Insight #67

FORGIVENESS OF SELF

There is no pill, no lotion, no potion, no energy balancing, no psychic reading, and no affirmation that can change what was. As light shines into darkness, so love brings warmth and peace to the blackest of blackest places. You have seen some black places. This is true for all. Forgiveness of self is the key to accessing the light. Forgiveness of others is noble; yet forgiveness of self must come first.

One of the greatest gifts I could give myself is the gift of self-forgiveness. What happened in the past has happened. The phrase, "no use crying over spilt milk" comes to mind. I could spend an entire lifetime whining and crying over milk I spilt. Let the past live in the past. The past cannot be removed. I may be able to change my perception or the significance of the past, but that does not change the event.

Love and self-forgiveness bring peace to those dark places I hide within myself. Guilt, shame, and blame fall into the category of dark places.

The key to letting light into my heart is forgiveness of self. What a joy to rid myself of the guilt, shame, and blame I allowed to be my truth. I tortured myself long enough. It is time to admit I made mistakes and now is the time to let go. Oh, what joy to be free of the choking and burdensome weight of these emotions!

I have witnessed people freeing themselves from their self-made weights by declaring, "I forgive myself for_____." Upon completing the act of forgiveness toward themselves they said, "Thank you, I am free now." Try it.

I remember being a participant in a self-help workshop where we were led through an exercise to learn how to forgive others. I had no problem with this. I understood people make mistakes and I was willing to forgive. However, when the facilitator began instructing us on the next exercise, which was self-forgiveness, I began to feel very uncomfortable. In fact, I was downright beside myself. It seems it was all right for other people to make mistakes, but whoa Nelly, I was not allowed to make them. Right there, on that day, after much wailing and beating pillows, I finally forgave myself for mistakes I made. I set myself free. It was one of the most uplifting experiences I ever felt. I never realized how much I beat myself up for my past until I chose to let it go.

I know I made mistakes. These mistakes brought me to the point I am now, seeking higher ideals. The past was merely a step to propel me forward. I forgive and let go of the past now, then I step into the present. The present offers far more wisdom, truth and light than the past ever could.

There are people in my past who have done me great injustices. It is important to forgive them, but I must forgive myself first. It is only possible for me to access love for another, and thereby access forgiveness, when I act in a loving manner towards myself and forgive the choices I made.

Offering forgiveness to myself creates a freeing of my energies. Those demons that haunted me and dwell secretly in my present are finally put to rest. This allows space for new, higher vibration energy to enter. As a result, I am more aware of the love, harmony, and peace all around me. I gain a more fulfilled, rewarding, exciting, and loving life by being able to forgive, me.

It took time to let go of the past. I forgive myself. I allow the love and light I so desperately want in my life a chance to manifest. I forgive myself. I deserve it.

Do you have any dark places inside you that need light?

Insight #68

FORGIVENESS

Make a list of all the decisions, actions, and thoughts for which you feel you need to forgive yourself. You need not show this to anyone. These are yours. After you have written as many as you feel you can, write across each one, "I forgive myself." Not with the attitude of "what a fool I am" nor with the attitude of "this is an exercise I am doing because I read about it" but rather with a heartfelt joy of knowing you are letting go of unnecessary baggage. Send yourself a hug for each one and let it go. You will begin to create a new you. Once you have forgiven yourself, you have the power to forgive others.

It has to be one of the most difficult choices to make. The choice to forgive can be a gut wrenching, painful experience. I have witnessed people attempt to forgive and it is not an easy thing to watch. I wonder to myself why it is so hard to forgive.

I believe the answer is - if I let go by the act of forgiveness, whomever I forgive has won. If I forgive them for the terrible deeds they have done to me, their sentence is over. I do not want their sentence to end. I have given them a life sentence for the hurt they heaped upon me.

For me to forgive, it must come from my heart not my head. It must be a loving choice. It is extremely difficult to think lovingly or act in a loving manner toward someone I despise. It just does not seem right to be sending love to, or even feeling love for, someone who has done me wrong.

By holding on to that hate and anger, I allow the person power over me. They are still in my head, still arouse my anger, and still inflict pain when I think about them. They still have power over me.

By forgiving them, I become powerful. I say to those who caused me great pain, they no longer have power over me. I am setting them free and setting myself free at the same time.

My forgiveness is not about condoning what a person did. It is not about agreeing with or accepting the choices they made. It is about coming to the realization that holding on to this angry, dark energy is not in my best interest. Those who wronged me will have to wrestle with their own demons. Upon forgiving them, I defeat my demons and call in my higher energies.

I forgive myself and then I forgive others. When I do this, I own my power. I can't emphasize enough how important forgiveness of self and others is. It is a huge step in moving forward, to allow in love and remove guilt, anger, hate and all the other emotions that prevent us from being our God-like selves.

Insight #69

THE JOURNEY

Busy yourself creating what you want. What gifts, what contribution will you make for mankind? Other endeavors are fine AND the focus of your energies would be best spent moving toward your goals. Your goals, your dreams, have already been created. Now go towards them. Your vision is already made. The results are there. It's your dreams, your goals and everyone is at the finish line waiting for you to arrive. It is the journey, not the result that will enlighten you. So begin.

I walk through life (ok stumble through life) not knowing where the heck I am going or what I am doing. It is important for me to create what it is I want. There are no rules saying I cannot have... the only exception to this is I cannot have what I believe I cannot have. When I speak of things I can have, I am talking about anything I want. It could be health, wealth, loving relationships, and the job of my dreams (writing a book) or perhaps not having a job. Whatever it is I want will come to me much faster when I am focused and "on purpose." This is when I have a clear vision of who I am and what I want to accomplish.

I am perfectly clear I want to write this book. The purpose for writing this book is people who read it would have an opportunity to understand more about personal and spiritual growth. Upon beginning to write (action), I attract the energy and circumstance that will assist me in completing this project. When I am not on purpose and have no direction or focus, I will not be able to attract the energy necessary to expedite the finished book. My scattered energy weakens attraction levels.

What contribution do I want to give the world? When I speak of the world, I do not mean I need to become famous worldwide, but rather I want to be "on purpose" in every moment. Every choice and decision carefully made with the following question in mind, "Does this compliment who I say I BE?"

The key is to be clear about who I am and what I want to give. If you don't know who you are and what you want to give, answer this question: **What is missing in this world?** Think about it. Now put this book down for a moment and ask yourself the question again. What is missing in this world? Write down your answer.

Whatever you said is missing in this world is a clue to what your life's purpose is all about. What was it you said? What is missing? It is not really missing in this world, but it is missing in you. Somewhere - whatever word you said - is missing in you. Now you get to be the creator of whatever you see missing. For me it was lack of love and ever since, I have been learning and teaching about love, at whatever level I am capable of understanding. I do not profess to know all there is. In fact, the more I say I know, the more I realize how little I know. I know perhaps only a small portion about love, but I made it my life's purpose to be of love and to teach love. That does not mean I am perfect.

Whatever we do and wherever we go we get to be the creator of what is missing in our life. If you understand and accept what I just wrote, you have just started a new journey.

The next paragraph of this Insight, *"Your goals, your dreams, have already been created. Now go towards them. Your vision is already made. The results are there."* This is not talking about pre-destiny. It is not saying my life is all mapped out. It is talking about the power of thought and the manifestations of such. Each of my thoughts carries energy. All energy manifests (a final result). This Insight tells me my goals and dreams are already created. It's as though the Universe is one-step ahead of me, waiting for me to catch up. The thoughts and dreams I have allow for this pre-manifestation. My thoughts have energy and by having thoughts I begin to attract the manifestation of these thoughts. My thoughts have real energy and power. Thus, by thinking in a certain way I attract the manifestations of those thoughts. My vision is created because I created the vision. The results exist because they are the results of my thoughts. So, what's in the way? Action and receptivity. It takes action to manifest a thought. A thought alone has energy, but the action of that thought .... the "doing" of the thought allows for a manifestation - the result.

The last paragraph talks about the journey and not the results will enlighten me. It is from the **experiences** and reality I create along the way that gives me wisdom. If I receive a paycheck every two weeks and don't remember the work I did to get that paycheck, the paycheck would have no significance. It has no energy. It is simply money. If I were at the finish line of life without remembering my work, my life would not have any significance.

So, start the journey you want to begin. Start today.

Insight #70

YOUR SHOPPING CART

Continue along your path placing in your shopping cart of life what you choose to be appropriate. If you find items in your cart you no longer wish to have, you may place them back on the shelf. If other people put items in your cart that are not in harmony with what you want, you may choose to remove those items. You don't have to pay for another's goods. Let them pay for their own shopping, their own choices.

Oh how I like this Insight. It makes life appear as if I am in a department store on a continual shopping journey. What fun. What I put in my cart is what I have in my life. How cool is that?

This means I have total choice about what I put in my life. I choose it. I attract it, and accept it as mine. If at any point I no longer choose to have an item in my cart, I can put it back on the shelf. I can return it or exchange it. I can do this as often as I wish.

Other people may find useful items for me too and place them in my cart. Now this is cool. People can assist me in shopping. I do not have to do it all alone. However, if someone places something in my cart I really do not wish to be in there, I can remove those items.

Wow! I think about all the "stuff" people put in my cart and much of it I don't want, but I shop with it anyway because they put it there. How dumb is that?

Some people even put stuff in my cart that is not even for me. They just want me to carry it around and pay for it. It's not even mine. Yes, let them pay for their own goods, their own choices. I am only going to pay for mine.

Insight #71
DISTRACTION

Avoidance, procrastination, chaos, drama, depression, anger. Are any of these distracting you from your dream, your purpose? Once again, you need to look at your commitment and refocus on what you are committed to. Know there are those around you who want and wait to assist you moving toward your dream, your goal. You must make yourself, your desires, dreams, and purpose known to others before they will appear. Are you willing to let others assist you?

There are many ways I distract myself from moving toward my goals, dreams, and life purpose.

I create chaos so there is not enough time in the day to do all the things I want to do. I am constantly late, forgetting appointments, rushing here, rushing there. I handle too many crises. It always seems I am putting out some kind of fire. There is no time for a holiday. I always have to do just one more thing. I am always running behind and never caught up. I am never finished and I am never complete.

I procrastinate. When I am not in chaos I procrastinate, which in turn leads to chaos. I say I really want to complete something, but something comes up and I do not get it done. Sometimes I can be just plain lazy.

I avoid. Avoidance is similar to procrastination. I do not want to look. I move away from the task at hand. I close my eyes and hope it will go away. I don't want to deal with what is at hand because it feels overwhelming. There is a big pile of items to deal with. Some of these items I just choose not to pay attention to until…. they become part of the chaos.

I create drama. Drama is similar to chaos. I involve myself in my own or other's catastrophes. I, or those around me, appear to be in constant crisis. Other people require so much energy and attention I forget about my own needs and desires.

I can be burnt out. This is when I do not have the drive or desire to do anything. I am plain worn out. I cannot take it anymore.

I can be angry. I feel angry with myself. I feel angry with co-workers and family members. I even exhibit anger in my recreational time. I want to shout out. I want everyone to smarten up and get his or her act together. "Why doesn't anyone listen? Why don't they get it? If only _____, I would not feel so angry."

If you have experienced any of these acts or emotions, they are signs you are pulling yourself away from your goals and dreams. Stop! Take inventory. What is your life about? What do you want? Are you being pulled away from your path?

It is time I commit or recommit to myself. What is it I am committed to? Who am I and what do I stand for? Know I am not alone. I do not have to struggle by myself to reach my goals, dreams, and life purpose. There are people who I can attract to myself to assist me along the way. The more I stay focused on what I want, the quicker those people will show up to assist me.

To help me attract the right people along my path I must make my goals, dreams, and life purpose known to others. I must speak it. Tell others. I become like a promoter or salesman enrolling people into my life because they **want** to assist me. I must ask and be ready to receive. Am I willing to let others assist me?

Insight #72

LOVE

Know there is only one Love. The Love of God. Not as a separate entity, but as a way of being. Not the way Love should look, but the way it is. There is only Love.

I must admit I feel inadequate when speaking about Love. Many writers and poets speak of love far more eloquently than I do. There is only one Love. That is the Love of God. There is only one Love. There is only Love. God creates and created from a place of Love and continues to do so today. All entities are experiencing Love, albeit some are on a different level. Love is the only energy that survives.

Love is the unselfishness of assisting another to love. It is the only survival quality. When the body has been cast aside, it is only love that continues to be.

Love is not a separate entity. I do not have a monopoly on Love. And, it is impossible to be devoid of love, for it is from that which we were created. Love is a way of being. It is a way of understanding those around us and the struggles they encounter, without going into judgment mode or trying to rescue. I cannot control another's experience or their exploration and heightened awareness of Love.

The bottom line is only to love. No matter what level anyone is in life, we are all surrounded by the Love of the Universe, the love of God. It is only my limiting beliefs about what love looks like that prevents me from accessing that love and sharing it with others.

I often hear what love is not, but seldom do I hear what love is. I choose to make my life one of love. I allow those around me to love and be loved and I allow those around me to love me.

The greatest and saddest of all my errors either is to refuse to receive love or refuse to give love.

Insight #73

IMPERFECTION

Do not beat yourself up for what you perceive in yourself to be imperfect. You are being trained, to be a master, a leader, a changer of ways. Allow your feelings of imperfection and inadequacy to come to the surface for they are fears to be overcome.

I have noticed I am not perfect. I have made mistakes (I know that's hard for some of you to believe). I have done things so stupid, so dumb, and so moronic I say to myself, "Why the heck did I do that?" These imperfections have remained in my consciousness forever and a day.

I could make a list of my imperfections. They might be a mile long or should that be, a smile long? I can look in the mirror and see my current imperfections and I can well remember my past imperfections.

Imperfections as I see them are a perception. The incident that created the imperfection was a neutral event. It had no significance. It only gained significance when I gave it such. Each one of us seeing or having the same experience (the same neutral event) may have chosen to give it a different significance. One of us might have thought the experience funny while another chose to be angry.

Imperfection is a perception. The athlete who tries a fancy move, loses his balance, and ends up with his butt on the ground is not imperfect. He was doing, he was creating, experimenting, pushing, risking, and he was magnificent. What he says about his butt on the ground is his perception and he chooses the significance to this neutral event.

At times (all too often), I have made the fancy move and landed square on my butt too. I can choose to sit there and whine about how I got there and how it was not fair, or how it was a stupid move to make or I can get up and say, "WOW! THAT WAS AN EXPERIENCE. NEXT TIME I AM GOING TO..."

Feelings of imperfection are not to be squashed. They are a sign I am experiencing fear. Feelings of imperfection can be overcome by understanding the fear behind them. The athlete who lands on his butt has a fear he is not good enough. The athlete needs to overcome his fear (perception of himself) of not being good enough. What is important is the fear of not being good enough must be removed from his consciousness. The athlete has a choice as to what importance (the significance) he places on what happened. It is what the athlete chooses to believe about the experience, that gives him his power.

It is important for the concept of imperfections to surface. Understanding and being in touch with the underlying fear that has been programmed into oneself is critical in moving forward. Fear is the greatest obstacle in moving forward.

I once read if you knew everything was going to turn out perfectly, what would you do? I thought about that and decided I would go for it right now, this minute. The only thing stopping me from going 100% forward was fear of failure.

Put aside fear and it is full speed ahead. So it is for all fears. They can be acknowledged and discarded like a powerless demon. Then all the power to become perfect, to be successful, is for the taking.

Insight #74

ALL SOULS

*Do you find it hard to speak, to show love? For you have only touched that place for fleeting moments. Yet, this is enough to show others. Know, in all people you judge to be either "this" type or "that" type lays a perfect soul. No matter what anyone says, **ALL** souls are perfect.*

There have been moments in my life where I felt love. There has been a feeling of complete peace. I experienced a feeling of belonging, a joyous peace and a vibrant quietness, knowing everything is in its rightful place. To have been touched by this love is enough for me to communicate to others about the love that is possible yet, reality seems such a chaotic and disruptive place survival takes precedence over expression and communication of giving and receiving love.

Occasionally, there are people who enter my space who seem bent on destruction. They create chaos and confusion. These people appear to be selfish, sexist, ignorant, violent, abusive, racists, and bigots. I tell myself if they would only go away, my life and the lives of many others would be better off.

The concept that everyone is perfect no matter how it appears, is somewhat disturbing. There are souls who appear to be less than God-like. There are those who seem to have no respect for God, or my fellow man.

All humans, whether rich or poor, male or female, be they any nationality or any religion, have the potential to be God-like. Each human has within them the spark of God; it is this spark, which separates us from all other creatures. We have the freedom to choose to be God-like, to love one another. This is the gift of free will.

Inside each one of us is God waiting for us to synchronize our minds and hearts with Him. This only comes through conscious choice and service.

It is up to each of us to reach out and project our love to all whom we meet. It just may be our true giving of love, allows another soul the chance to look at love differently. Perhaps I can assist another on their journey by my willingness and desire to love them.

All souls are perfect, but they sure have a funny way of showing it. They are perfect because they have the God-spark within them. They all have the opportunity to be God-like.

Oh yes, All SOULS, no exceptions.

Insight # 75
DISAPPEARANCE OF SELF

The disappearance of self can be returned in a millisecond to a state of love. The decision to choose love instead of selfishness returns the soul on its journey to its creator. Can you show others how to see the light, to see Love? You do not have to carry them on your back forever and a day; just show them what you know in your heart to be true. They may resist what you speak, for you challenge them to return to a place where they can't remember the love within.

I have a self. It is unique to me. Not one is exactly alike. I may share many similar attributes and qualities, but no two of us is exactly the same. This individuality, along with the gift of free will, allows me the choice to stray from the path. That path is choosing love. There are times when life gets in the way of choosing to be the highest I can be. Life happens and living in a chaotic place where I am constantly in survival mode causes me to forget the higher meaning of my existence.

Some decisions I make are selfish in nature. Some are out of Love. I will question myself the next time I make a decision: What are my motives? I will ask myself why I am choosing to make such a decision. Is it out of fear? Is it out of selfishness, or out of love?

I am surrounded by Love. Within me (and you) is the spirit of God. This is Love and it lives within us. I cannot always see or feel it. I cannot always hear it speak to me. Yet it is there, always guiding me, energizing me to make the highest possible choices. This does not mean I always make the highest choices, I am constantly fed God's spirit in hopes I will choose the highest.

There is no ledger listing the mistakes I make, but I believe there is a record of the higher choices I make. I can choose, at any time, to put all my mistakes behind me. I can choose, at any time, to do the will of the Father. I can choose, at any time, to put selfishness aside and choose selflessness. I can choose, at any time, to be more God-like. I can choose, at any time, to be more loving to all I meet. BUT I HAVE TO CHOOSE! It is by choosing my direction and who I am going to BE that I am given the blessing of the Higher Spirit. The decision to choose Love instead of selfishness allows the inflow of the Higher Spirit. It allows one to access the God-spirit that lives within. By choosing love and working in harmony with my in-dwelt God- spirit, I begin a journey that will take me to God.

As I choose the path of being a person of light and love, I have the opportunity to show others this beauty. Showing them the love I have, will allow them the opportunity to choose the same. As I have a choice from my indwelt God-spirit to have light and love, so does everyone else. If a person can see how loving I am, they have a better concept of what it means to choose love and to be in love.

People may resist my love. They may not return the love I give. This is not important. What is important is I continue to shine, continue to give my love. I must remember I have not always been a person of love (and I have so much more to learn), and there are those out there who are not quite ready to make decisions that will lead them back to their Creator – at least not yet.

Insight #76

CHOOSING A GOD

Those who turn to God out of fear, choose a God who creates fear. Their lives are fear based. They have chaos and turmoil. Those who turn to God out of Love, create a God of Love. Their lives are Love based. They have peace and harmony.

I choose which God I follow. I can choose the God of Love or I can choose the God of Fear. The God of Fear is a fear based God. If I follow this God, honor this God, and believe this is my God, this God will be real. I will create a life of chaos and fear. The God I choose to identify myself with is the God who will lead me.

If I identify myself as one who fears God, I will surely create manifestations that prove myself right. I create my own reality based on what I believe to be true.

If I can believe God is Love, I will most certainly create manifestations that prove myself right. I create my own reality based on what I believe to be true.

I choose the God of Love. Which God do you choose?

Insight #77

PSYCHICS

*Be aware of those who call themselves "psychic" or "mediums." They only see what is in **their** reality. The same energies read by two different psychics would render "readings" different from the other. Each would "read" based on their own reality. All "readings" are true, but only from the viewpoint (their reality) of the person giving the "reading." Know the truth, the way, the future, the past, is all within you to create. To allow another to speak of your future, they only speak of the present (with the future based on your present). You have the power to change your present, thus changing your future. Nothing is set. You always have choice. Remember this.*

I used to believe everything I do or everything that happens is set in motion long before it actually occurs. I thought the triumphs and tragedies that befall us were predetermined. I visited psychics in an attempt to gain foresight or knowledge into future events. But as the Insight reads, psychics only have the ability to "see" based on what they have seen.

Let me explain. If a psychic had never seen broccoli in their life, how would it be possible for them to say broccoli is a good choice for my dinner?

If a psychic had never been in a loving relationship, how would it be possible for them to know my relationship will be a loving one? They may say I am going to be in a loving relationship, but this can only be based on what the psychic knows as love in their own reality.

If ten psychics tell me I am going to have a loving relationship with another person, each one would be basing this prediction on what they personally see as a loving relationship. This prediction can only be offered from what they have found to be a loving relationship. There is no guarantee just because they predict it; I am going to be in a loving relationship. The psychic's prediction may not fit in to what is my ideal of a loving relationship.

The same is true for money and wealth. If the psychic predicts I will be rich, this information is based on what the psychic's standard of wealth is to be considered rich. Reality is I may or may not be wealthy; this depends on where I set my marker, not on what the psychic considers the mark.

Whatever a psychic says, they are only reading a probability of what is likely to happen based upon my present. They can only predict the future based upon the present, my present. For example, the psychic may say I will have a long, loving relationship with my partner; however, at any given moment either partner may choose to end the relationship.

No matter what any psychic says, I always have the opportunity to create my future based upon my choices. Nothing is set. I ALWAYS have a choice. Thus, my future is always mine to create.

Insight #78

FORTUNE TELLERS

Those who foretell the future, those who "tune in" without spiritual attunement, those who channel without love, create fear, havoc, and chaos. It is an energy misused. Beware of those who only have their own intentions at stake. Know you have the answers inside you. Be still and listen; the answers you seek will be given.

From the very young age of thirteen, I had the opportunity to be with and experience many fortunetellers. I seemed to be entranced with them and them with me. They were impressed with my being so curious and full of desire to learn about the metaphysical at such a young age. It seemed as though everyone I met was doing some sort of "reading." Some were in to "reading" past lives. Some were in to healing the physical body. Some were in to The New World Order, and some seemed a bit weird, like the lady who sacrificed her cat and then wanted to do hands on healing for me. "Ummm no thanks… I have to go now." I received a boatload of past life readings. Yet, I question today why no two psychics ever spoke of the same past life I may have had. I would think if one particular life was of such importance to me, numerous psychics would make mention of this, yet in all my readings no psychic ever mentioned any past lives other psychics went into detail about.

I also had psychics read my future. Since I was not receiving any blinding flashes of revelations at that time (age thirteen to eighteen), I went to those who seemed able to touch a place I could not. I went to them looking for answers. At that time, I believed in pre-destiny. I learned, after visiting numerous psychics over the years, there are those who seem able to tap into a place of higher consciousness. It was as though a higher self or God-like energy was speaking to them. These readings empowered me to strive to be more passionate about my life, my purpose, and my goals. They spoke of the power of love and joy of service. I always left feeling as if nothing was concretely answered; yet, I knew I had a new perspective on life. I believed a Higher Source had a very definite plan for me and it was my choice how I would manifest it.

In fairness to psychics, they simply provide information. What I choose to do with that information, and the decisions I make around that information, is me creating my reality.

Imagine you and your significant other go to a psychic on different days, at different times. The psychic says you are going to live to the grand old age of 95; however, your significant other is told he or she is going to live until age 60. You now believe you will live 35 years without your significant other. How would you feel? Empowered? Are you ready to be passionate about life and walk forward with great enthusiasm? How will you feel when your significant other approaches the age of 60? Would you feel fear when you think about losing your loved one? How many years have you been building that fear knowing your significant other is approaching death? If it is predestined you will live until you are 95, there is no way you can exit early. Do you, knowing you are going to live to 95, think you can walk in front of moving cars because the psychic said you would live to the age of 95? Of course not!

A good psychic will not map out your life or tell you specifics on how or what your life should be. A good psychic will point you in a direction, assist you in seeing your strengths, empower you with love, and touch your heart. A good psychic will show you that you have numerous choices.

A psychic who misuses this energy is tuned in without caring for the soul. Without spiritual attunement, they will create readings that render fear. Such readings do not come from a place of Love.

Finally, there is no need to go to a psychic. Ever! All the answers I ever want and need are inside me. The God spirit (far greater than any fortunetellers limited insights) is right with me, **ALL THE TIME**. I can ask whatever questions I wish and all I have to be is still enough to hear the answers. I have to be still to listen.

Insight #79

CHOICE

If you choose to have or want something in your life and also want other things in your life, there is no reason to deny yourself either. The Universe is a provider of all things, not a limited few. All things can be manifested depending on how you choose. You must ask and be clear on what you want; otherwise, you become a victim of your own indecisions. Chaos and confusion will be created when intentions are not clear. Know what you want and choose it. You have the gift of free will. Nothing is set. You always have choice and you will always receive what you are committed to having.

Sometimes I feel when I am presented choices I must choose one way or the other. Is it possible I can have both? The Universe is willing to provide me with anything and everything, providing it is in my best interests to have it. I must be clear on what I ask. I need to be a laser guided missile to my target. I must visualize and set the steps in motion to receive. I must prepare the way. I think back to things I asked for ... heck, I don't need to think back, I can think right now - and it seems I don't always get what I ask for. Why is it I believe giving me more of something will rid me of problems? If I can't manage what I have, won't more just make it worse? If I can't manage my money while having small amounts, how am I going to manage big amounts? If I can't manage the small amount of love I receive, how am I going to receive buckets full? If I am uncomfortable giving out small words of appreciation, how am I going to give out pounds of it? Won't I be more uncomfortable?

Asking is like ordering from a menu. In the restaurant of life where I am for the moment (pretend with me), I have only a vague idea of what to order. My conversation would go like this, "Umm, I'd like something that has taste and makes me feel good." The waiter scurries off to deliver my order. But... I change my mind while the waiter is away and as I see the waiter in the distance I say to him, "Umm, I'd like the very best you have please." "Yes, you may have this," the waiter responds, "and exactly what Best are you talking about?"

"I don't know. Just give me the best."

The waiter stands beside me waiting for more information so he can complete my order and I impatiently wait for it to arrive. My order finally arrives and the waiter proudly places the dishes in front of me. I begin to gag as I taste what he brought me, because this BEST is certainly not to my liking. This could never be what I ordered. I complain and say this is not what I want. The waiter says, "I sent you the Best, as requested." "But, I don't want this!" I exclaim. The waiter leaves the food on the table and says, "You ordered it, you have to pay for it, so deal with it."

I gather all the dishes from my table and place them in the garbage can. Again, I summon the waiter and make a request. "I would like chicken, please." The waiter goes off to bring my chicken. When he returns he has two chicken wings and places them at my setting. "What is this?" I ask, "I wanted chicken." "This is chicken," he replies. "Well, I wanted more chicken than this." He replies, "You did not request how much chicken you wanted; if you would like to order again you may."

And so it goes, in my restaurant of life. Somehow, I had the impression a higher power than me would just somehow know everything I wanted and provide me with it. So far, I am not convinced the Higher Power understands everything I desire and if the Higher Power does understand, it sure the heck is not giving it to me until I am mature enough to handle it.

Indecision, being unclear, expecting the Universe knows what I really want or need, often brings less than satisfactory results. Nothing is set. There is no higher force preventing me from accessing anything. It is my

own beliefs, my own indecision, my own immaturity, and self-created demons that prevent me from accessing what I want.

I need to be completely clear when I ask for something, requesting
exactly what it is I want. I always have choice. When I am committed
(action word) to having something I want and am willing to take action to
create what I want, it will always manifest.

Insight #80

LISTENING

There is a need for you to listen. Know you need the discipline of being still and meditating. A quieting of the mind. The way you listen at this moment in time is similar to being on the receiving end of a phone conversation while having your television or stereo volume up very loud. The outside or background interference prevents you from hearing or being fully aware. There is too much noise in your head. Take time to be still, to listen, and to write, every day. If you will be but still and listen, wonders will unfold for you!

The discipline of quieting my mind is a very useful tool in spiritual and personal awakening. This does not necessarily mean I sit in the lotus position (torturing myself) chanting mantras. Any attempt at sitting in a cross-legged position will have me focusing on the desire for a masseuse or a chiropractor. When I meditate, I take time to listen to the little voice within. I may just close my eyes in a comfortable chair and ask a question. I always take a question into meditation. I listen for the response. It is about stopping in this chaotic world and taking a time out - to listen.

I have to admit I am not the worlds best at meditation. I am easily distracted and become easily uncomfortable, but when I do feel the urge to sit and be still, it is always a pleasant and rewarding experience. I listen to my inner self, my higher self, my God, when meditating. I have tried to listen with my inner stereo turned up loud. Listening when there is simply too much outside noise does not work for me. I cannot listen with all the chatter inside as well. I have to clear space for the God influence.

I cannot listen to God and listen to all the outside noise at the same time. Quieting my mind is being conscious that I can slow down, relax, and turn within. My meditations take the form of listening while I am taking a shower, driving a car, lying in bed looking at the ceiling, walking along a quiet path, sitting beneath a tree, getting close to nature, listening to a soothing environmental tape, etc. Meditating is about relaxing, stilling the outside world so it is quiet enough to listen, to become creative, and allow for the opportunity to hear higher thoughts, higher wisdoms.

I allow myself the freedom and easiness to make time to be still and listen.

Insight #81

CREATING

Put all your wants on paper. These are your creations. Do not keep them in your head. Write all of them down on paper. Be clear what you ask for. The clearer or more visually committed you are, the greater the speed of manifestation. You may demand whatever you want. Have you thought about how you want your spiritual world to look?

There is something powerful about writing what it is I want on a piece of paper. Writing down my desires has more power than simply storing them in my head (If you had my memory you would know why I write them down). I thought about why this might be. When I write, I visualize what I want. The whole time I am writing (which generally takes longer than speaking), I am creating "pictures" in my mind. I am creating the vibration energy that allows me to attract what I am asking for.

Writing, "I demand to have a new car" ten times has me imagining what this car looks like. It becomes more than a repetition of words. I have always thought (and still do) the constant repetition of words in mantras or affirmations is entirely useless UNLESS, the mantras and affirmations are combined with a visual. Words have more when they are combined with visuals and accompanying energizing feelings.

Just thinking about a desire or want is not enough. I must be willing to allow the energy of this desire or want to become a movie in my head. The clearer the movie, the better the manifestations of that want. I must "see" what I am demanding. I must feel the benefit of what it is I am asking for.

Being clear as to what I am asking for is very important. I have been known to ask for something rather general, hoping some magical power will fill in all the details and give me what I really want. I remember demanding a new car but I did not bother to go into detail. I asked for a car that would be sound, have a stereo, and be affordable etc. Secretly I was hoping the Universe would surprise me with this super duper looking car that would turn people's heads and show me as a successful person. I did not want to appear greedy, so I just asked for a car. Alas, with mixed messages I ended up with guess what?

I ended up with a reliable four door General Motor's product that was certainly not going to turn any heads. If anything, it would turn heads away. I did not feel the least bit like a show off or successful businessperson in this car. I did get what I asked for. I certainly did not get what I wished for **secretly**.

Before choosing to move to a new home, my family always writes down what they want in the new home. Picture, if you will, four small bodies ranging in ages from 5-11 and two adult bodies gathered at the kitchen table making a list of what we want in our new house. Number of bedrooms, patio, deck, sunlight, number of bathrooms, office space, hot tub, quiet, close to everything, price, the date we would take possession, etc. When we were done, there were over 35 items on our list. At one point when we were creating our list we all closed our eyes and visualized what the house would look like. Of course, every one of us visualized it differently, but the cooperative energy was enough to manifest it within a couple of weeks.

We have received many houses this way and the last house we pictured we received all but two items. One item we did not get was an ocean view; however, we can walk to the ocean in under 5 minutes. The other item we did not get was a hot tub; we settled for a Jacuzzi tub in the bathroom. We forgot to ask for some things because we took them for granted. Guess what? We did not get them. We did not ask for cable TV because everyone has it, well, everyone but us. We did not ask for sparkling clear water.

Occasionally, it turns a rusty brown depending on the water level. I must remember not to take anything for granted when asking for what I want.

Once I decide and am clear about what I want off the Universe menu, I can order my meal and the cooks get busy and create it for me. My server brings me eating utensils and my meal to the table. It is up to me to act, by picking up the fork and eating the food before me. When it comes to what I desire in life: I ask for what I want. I accept the tools given me and proceed ahead.

I can demand whatever I want. I am the creator. I am the power supply. I am the generator. I decide what I have in my life. But, I have to ask for it.

I am constantly thinking about how I would like my spiritual and emotional world to look. Again, I am the creator, I am the power. I can create whatever I want in my life. The rules are the same for spiritual, emotional, and physical wants. I create by writing down, speaking, seeing, and receiving what I want. I sit for a moment and visualize how my ideal world looks. Then, I write it down and ask that it be so.

Creating is about asking for and being open to receiving what I have asked for.

Insight #82

BECOMING AWARE

Become aware of those people around you. Those you come in contact with. You have already become more aware you create your own reality. People do not arrive in your reality on some cosmic chain of predestined circumstances. You must learn to see, to feel, to love, and create them. They are in truth, a part of you.

The previous Insight was how to create possessions. First, I must have a clear intention and vision to have these things.

The Becoming Aware Insight is about creating people.

The people I had in my life, the people I have in my life, and the people I will have in my life are all created by me. I know this because my thoughts and beliefs have created the people who are now around me.

I attract people. I create them. I do not believe in soul mates. There is no "right" match. There simply is the experience of another soul. I see so many people looking for their soul mate. They desperately seek their other half. There is no right person. There simply is a person.

Do I approve of the people I have around me? Are they loving people I would choose to walk with on my path of life? If yes, this is great. If not, here are some clues on how I bring people I want to me.

It works the same way as creating "things." The only difference is I want to create the experience, not the person. Let's say I want to work in an environment where there is love and harmony. I don't "create" Mr. Joe Happiness in my head, I create the experience. I imagine myself welcomed with open arms, I imagine myself being productive and very useful, being a part of the larger picture. I imagine those around me supporting me in my decisions and me supporting them. I don't create the person; I create the experience (and I write down the experience I am looking for).

An example of creating the experience would be... hmmm. Let's say I wanted the experience of marrying Cindy Crawford (the world famous model). I could visualize her forever and ever, see us getting married and the whole life scene together; however, it may and most probably would never happen (so far it has not happened). Why? Because she gets to create people she wants in her life too. If she's not creating me, we shan't be together (her loss). Creating Cindy is also a form of control. I am placing another person on a path where she may not want to go. This is control.

To create the right experience I would find all the things I am attracted to in Cindy, and ask for an **experience** with those qualities be created or attracted to me. I want a fun loving, confident, happy go lucky, slim figured female who makes friends easily, and wants a long lasting committed relationship (WITH ME). This I can ask for because now, I have asked for the experience, not a specific person. I also must believe I can have it. I have now sent out the energy of what I want to create and I must wait for it to manifest. Just sitting at home won't work. What steps do I need to take to bring this about? What is my next step after creating the experience of what I am looking for?

I know any person who is in my life was created through my thoughts, beliefs, and actions. I create the experience of this person. If I want to change the type of people I attract, I have to visualize a new type of people, a new experience. If I do this, I will find relationships that don't fit in to my new vision, will fade away, sometimes with conflict, sometimes without.

I and I alone am accountable for the type of relationships I have. I and I alone am the one with the power to change any relationship. It is I that must change, not the other people. I only have the power to change me.

Insight #83

HEALING

There is before you an avenue of healing. This is about to manifest (the avenue). This is for your own healing. To be healed- to heal oneself- is to be set free. It is time to step into a new realm.

Today, more than any other time in human history, there is the availability of different avenues for healing. Whether I need physical or emotional healing, there are numerous choices before me to try.

There is an avenue of healing about to manifest or to show itself to me. Since I am not a psychic, this Insight would be better read as: There is an avenue of healing before me. I must look for and become aware of it.

Personally, I believe all physical ailments have an emotional cause. Without getting into a huge discussion on this topic, for which I am highly unqualified, I suggest you check your local bookstore; it has numerous books on how to help you heal your body and mind.

No one can heal me. I must make choices, choose avenues, and manifest people who will coordinate my being healed; however, I can create the healing, I must first desire to be healed. The "healer" does not do the healing, the "patient" does. I ask for the manifestation of the most appropriate person(s) or avenue(s) to assist me in ridding myself of the "ailment." The healer could be a medical doctor, therapist, naturopath, acupuncturist, or any other type of avenue whereby promotion of health is paramount. The practitioner is simply the tool. They could work with me for many years, but it is not until I consciously agree to be healed that healing begins. By letting go of old hurts and negative experiences more energy is now available to aid in my healing. My sluggishness, depression, abundance of anger, and fear are all signs of old hurts and old personal stories that need to be healed. I choose to be healed and move into a new consciousness where there is less struggle and more victories, for I have cleared out the old and let in the new.

The power of how I live and how I choose to be healed is my choice.

Insight #84

WISHY WASHY

To wish for, is not enough. To hope for, means nothing. To demand has power! Demand what you want. Not as a wishy-washy wish. Demand! Not from anger. Demand! Not from fear, but from love. Is your asking, wishing? Demand with a higher purpose in mind. Start demanding what you want. Demanding or commanding has you own your power. You are the power. You choose. You demand.

You may have noticed in earlier Insights, I used the word demand rather than the word want when it comes to creating something, someone, or some experience. This writing explains why.

Demand? Now I thought to myself, that's an interesting concept. Demand? Who am I to demand? What makes me think I have the power to demand anything? I thought demand was pushy, forceful, and angry.

This Insight suggests I was being wishy washy in what I asked for. My asking was really wishing. It would go something like this. "Dear Universe, at this time I find myself in need of a transportation vehicle. If you can see your way to sending me one, that would be really nice of you. Thanks. Phil."

You can imagine the Universe receiving this and saying, "HMMM-MMM." There are millions of cars out there, all different shapes, sizes, colors, and quality. I wonder which one he wants. He wants us to decide for him because he doesn't know himself what he wants. The Universe files this away as "incomplete" and awaits further instructions or completes the deal as best possible.

Demanding is about being clear - what you want, why you want it, and what you want it for. It is about being clear and firm. It is as though, when you place your request, the result has already happened. There is no doubt to its manifestation. The energy necessary is the purpose, conviction and the **ACTION** to bring it about.

When ordering food at a restaurant I have a good idea what I want. I demand bacon and eggs. I demand the bacon crispy and the eggs over easy. I demand whole-wheat toast. I demand a glass of orange juice as my beverage. I am very clear. I do not say to the server, "I want some bacon and eggs with some bread and a beverage" and let her figure out the rest. If I did, the chances of me getting what I really want would be slim.

The clearer I am in asking for what I want the better my chances are of receiving it.

Insight #85

REACH

Reach for the highest you can imagine. You may demand whatever you want. Know you are the power and can create whatever you want. Put all your wants, that is, creations, on paper, for as you ask they are created.

This Insight is similar to the previous one with added information, when demanding anything it is important to ask for the highest I can imagine. For example, if I were demanding a loving relationship I must reach for the highest. I must visualize this loving relationship to the highest of my ability. Why would I want to do this? Not visualizing the highest would result in who knows what showing up on my doorstep.

If I ask the Universe for a loving relationship, it (the Universe) works with me to attract the person based on how I believe relationships work. If I have not thought in a higher way, I will not attract higher love. I will attract who knows what, because I have not been clear. It's similar to being wishy washy and just hoping the Universe knows and will supply what I want.

I create my own reality based on what I demand.

When I place my demands on paper, they are created on another level. The manifestation of these is always ready to present itself, but my own limiting beliefs get in the way, preventing it from happening. Using the example above, limiting beliefs in this case could be restricting my images to a certain ethnic or religious group. Even my own insecurities prevent me from taking the next ACTION step to make things happen. I make choices based on the highest concept I can. If I want a family, I would visualize to the highest of my ability how a family looks or how I want it to look. If I want a satisfying and rewarding career, I would reach for the highest I believe possible in creating that experience.

I have now been shown I can ask for whatever I want. I can demand whatever I want. I know I create my own reality. So why not create my reality at the highest possible level I can. I am only weakened by my own limitations, my own (dis)beliefs.

Insight #86

WILLINGNESS TO PLEASE

People pleasers. I have met them. I am one of them. I allow another's wants and needs to be more important than my needs and wants. It gives me great joy to please whomever or for whatever purpose I am asked. I believe this is what my life is about; I want to give to others. I was taught it is better to give than to receive. I was taught to think little of myself, as this was considered selfish.

Being a people pleaser, I live my life through the joys and triumphs of those around me. Seldom do I get to be the victor. Seldom do I have any accomplishments that are noticed. I pat myself on the back for the good deed I have done assisting another. They could have done it without me and perhaps should have.

My willingness to please others is noble and good, but I must assess why I am so quick to help others. Why am I being in service to this person? Is it because I am "supposed" to be doing it? Is it because I "should" do this or because I "want" to be doing it? Is it my life calling? Do I feel guilty in entertaining the thought of turning aside someone who appears to be in need?

When I pay attention to what my life purpose is (and that purpose is my choice), it may very well fit I am indeed to be of service to some... but not all. When my people pleaser addiction takes control of me, I find I create a life of service without any respect for my own personal needs, growth, and spiritual development. This is destructive. I too am part of God. I get to be part of the Creator. I give myself permission to be first.

Putting me first is difficult. It speaks of selfishness and ego but in fact, when I put myself first it allows me to create a clear vision of who I am. I can now pick and choose whom I want to assist by asking the question, "Does helping this person or organization fit into my life purpose?" There are a million ways I can expend my energy. I would be wise to spend my energy in the arena that attracts me most. That arena, is the arena wherein lies my passion.

My life flows more easily when I own my own power and aid those people consistent with my purpose and direction. My struggles disappear and everything good comes in abundance. Only I have the power to let go of people pleasing. I could burn myself out trying to please everyone (and have), I choose to say no and just focus in areas that support who I am. This is not from a selfish ME, ME, ME, point of view; rather, if I put myself first I am able to assist many others while I grow, too. The circle of giving and receiving continues.

For those of you who have no direction or purpose, stop and take time to listen. Sit quietly. Relax, and ask for answers to be given to you. You are constantly being given guidance. You can probably think of times you made a last second decision that seemed to come out of nowhere and you were saved from some sort of tragedy or it propelled you to success. This is you listening and acting on your intuition. Angels, spirit guides, God, the force, The Universe, call it what you will, but you were, for that moment, in touch with a higher energy, a higher knowing that assisted you in making a choice. The final decision and choice is always yours.

Listening to your intuition is not a big deal. You do it all the time. You do not need to see a thousand angels dancing in a blinding white light in front of you to hear a message. Just sit back and ask for an answer to be given. Then look for the answer. It may not be a voice in your head. It may be a physical in-your-reality clue. People pleasers, begin to put yourself first; in doing so you will be of far greater service, bringing more joy and love to many more people than you ever dreamed.

Insight #87

ARRIVING

People do not arrive on your path due to some cosmic chain of predetermined circumstances. They are created by you so you learn to feel, to see, to love. You choose what type of people you want in your life.

I stop and ask myself why certain people are in my reality. Do I ever consider myself lucky or fortunate to have "so and so" for a friend? I consider myself fortunate to have my life-partner. I also consider myself unlucky because numerous different, and not so pleasant people, cause me endless grief. Saying I am lucky and/or unlucky is giving away my power. It allows me to become a victim, the victim of luck, be it good or bad luck.

The people in my life, **without exception,** are there because I attracted them. Each person who crosses my path is there for only one reason. They are there to assist me in becoming the loving spirit I know I am. Let me explain.

First, look at the type of people with whom you enjoy being. These are people who support you, believe in you, and trust you. These people have come to assist you in seeing who you are. You create these people by asking consciously or unconsciously, to have love, friendship, and intimacy. The people you attract to yourself are manifestations of your thoughts, and beliefs. These friends are your choice. These friends and lovers, based on your belief system, are the best friends for you at this time. They are not gifts from the Universe. They are manifestations from you.

Second, look at the type of people you would rather erase from your life. These are people with whom you come in conflict. They offend, humiliate, anger, and embarrass you. These people are also present to assist you. Again, you created these people by asking consciously or unconsciously, to have people assist you in moving forward. These people mirror back to you all the weaknesses you perceive to have yourself. It is as if you could take a fear or negative belief and project it from inside you. What you end up with is the person you would rather not be with, you literally manifest your fears and attract people who show you those fears.

So, don't kill the messenger! When you find yourself in disharmony with another, take a note pad; write down what you do not like about them. Now realize these qualities reside in you and this messenger is making it clear to you. Now, you have the opportunity to remove these unwanted qualities from yourself. This could be in the form of forgiveness, auto-suggestion, affirmations, or whatever works for you. Just turn it around. Then the miracle happens. If you manage not to fight the messenger and do some inner cleansing, you will find the pain-in-the-butt person simply vanishes from your life. It is that simple. If the messenger hangs around, you haven't cleaned it all up yet.

About the Universe's role in this. The Universe is not sending you miserable, unhappy, controlling people to test you. The Universe is not setting you up. The Universe has not decided on such and such a day, in such and such a year - it is going to introduce you to a very difficult person. You decide who is in your life by your thoughts, beliefs, and actions. You control your reality.

Insight #88

100%

You may be going full out at 100%, using 100% of your energies; however, you are not giving 100%. Therein lies the answer to your shortcomings.

I asked myself, why the shorter the Insight the more pondering I must do to grasp its meaning? This Insight is in reference to me asking, why when I am going full out to make my financial life work, do I not seem to be making any progress? I spend more hours than I think I should making money. I use 100 percent of my energies. I am exhausted by the end of the day.

Surely, with all this expense of energy, I should have more. I should see more for all the toiling I am doing. When I reconcile at the end of the day it seems the amount of energy I put out, exceeds any gains coming in. I do not understand why this happens. It does not seem fair.

This Insight suggests I am going full out with 100 per cent of my energies, yet, part of the equation seems to be missing. That secret ingredient is the attitude of GIVING.

I had to ask myself, "What is GIVING?" The fact I did not know was a sign I was not giving, otherwise I would know what it was. Physical work is noble. Expending energy at work is expected. GIVING relates to my attitude and how I envision myself in my work area. I only viewed work as a way for me to create an income. After quietly thinking about GIVING, it dawned on me I was only conscious of TAKING from work. I viewed work as about me taking, rather than what I could give. I began to change my attitude and see work as a place of GIVING.

I changed my attitude so I viewed my work as something I contributed to others. I began to see how my work is something I GAVE rather than took, and it made work more exciting and rewarding. At work, I became part of the whole assisting the whole. I removed the ME being the whole. I began working for the good of all.

While my finances increased and stress levels went down, I still realize I have much more to learn. Giving to others requires constant vigilance. It's not hard for me to slip back into the "How much money can I make?" mentality without a thought of what I can give.

Insight #89

RESULTS

To do your best, and not finish first. Focusing on the end result and just the result means you may miss all the experiences along the way. The journey is where the joy is, where the wisdom penetrates your soul.

Results. That is quite often how I measure myself - by the results. If the results are what I set out to achieve, I consider myself a success. If the results are less than I set out to achieve, I consider myself a failure.

Many times I have embarked on a goal or project with as much enthusiasm and energy as I possibly could, and yet I come up short. The experience I choose is one of being a failure.

I have read books and listened to tapes and cd's on how to visualize what I want. These books Cd's and tapes inform me if I want that new car I have to visualize it. In my mind I must picture the make, model, and year, see myself in the driver's seat, see the gauges, get a feel for the interior, and so on. What I fail to recognize, in the time between conceiving the idea and creating the result, is the journey along the way. Simply receiving the car does not mean I am a success. It is the journey along the way that is important. This is where lessons and victories take place.

For example, **I decide I want to win a bicycle race**.

I could sit at home and visualize the perfect bike for my race. I could imagine my finely tuned machine performing without any flaws. I could picture myself effortlessly crossing the finish line arms raised in victory.

This is all fine and dandy; however, victory or defeat is not measured at the finish line, but rather by the amount of growth, learning, and wisdom I gain along the way. The real victory is in the journey of self-discovery, overcoming my blocks, fears, stories, and perceived weaknesses. If, when on my quest to become the champion cyclist I become more aware of who I am and get in touch with the synchronicity between my higher self and the physical me, it does not matter if I finish first or last. The victory is in learning, growing, and knowing.

If I am having trouble achieving the results I am looking for, perhaps it is time I stop focusing on results and start looking at the opportunities for growth that precedes any victory or failure.

Insight #90

CLOSER

*Often the closer you get to your goal the more ego fights you. Stay with your current project and learn from it. This may seem heavy now. Start visualizing how the finish will look. Enjoy the journey. Commitment **with joy** required.*

I noticed as I get closer to achieving a goal, the harder the going gets.

There are times when I have a clear vision of a goal I want to attain and I have a perfectly laid out plan to accomplish it. Along the way toward this goal, I stop, look around, and notice I am way off course. I say to myself, "How the heck did I get off course?"

Repeating this coming-up-short or failure habit numerous times (and I do mean numerous), made me realize I allow myself to be pulled off my path. I realized I would not allow feelings of jubilation and triumph to be part of my reality. As a result, I created dramas all around me that distracted me from my course, my path, my goals, and my life purpose, which resulted in my creations looking like a whirlwind of chaos.

I find goals much more easily attainable when I focus on the goal and allow feelings of contentedness, joy, excitement, and love to emerge. When I think of the journey as an exciting adventure rather than a difficult task, it becomes more fun.

Insight #91

GETTING CLOSE

You are getting close and ego is yelling at you to change course, to throw you off, not to allow the joyous feeling of triumph. Stay focused and don't let yourself or others pull you off your course. This is a distraction. Keep focused, joyous, content, excited, loving, and in harmony with Universal Laws.

My ego, the part of me that wants me to be safe and in my comfort zone, the part that wants to protect me from stepping outside my comfort zone is constantly talking to me. It reminds me of past failures and suggests the best course of action is for me to create something easier, something more in line with who I really believe I am.

Ego does all it can to keep me in the status quo, for ego knows that is where I am the most comfortable (even if it is uncomfortable).

As I get closer to a goal, closer to breaking through the ego and raising the bar on my comfort zone, ego gets loud and demanding and does everything in its power to keep me safe. It demands I not step out of place. It pulls me back. That is when chaos and drama show up, for ego knows that is when I can easily be swayed away from the higher or different choice I am making. If I can stay focused on the goal and not allow ego to sway me, I can attain my goal.

I allow myself to stay in integrity and clearly see my way to the finish line. I don't give up. I keep moving. I wade through difficulties and know when ego is screaming at me, I must be getting close. Now I can chuckle to myself because I know victory must be just around the corner.

Insight #92

WEIGHT

The "weight" you perceive is the "heaviness" you carry for not being the "super-man" you think you should be. Your "weight" is your emotional guilt. Many people carry the same "heaviness." It is time for you to refuel on an emotional level. Allow the light in. For light is fuel for the soul. Be still and refuel.

When speaking of weight here, it is not meant to be about body weight, although for some it may be.

When I have emotional guilt (I have been known to carry it around with me) it feels heavy. I might as well be dragging a sack behind me. I feel tired and many things that should be easily attended to, just feel like one thing too much. As a result, not much is accomplished and this adds further to the feeling of emotional guilt. Guilt can also be synonymous with other emotions - shame, blame, fear, sadness, etc.

My emotional guilt has usually revolved around not being a "perfect parent." Can anyone relate? Carrying this around does absolutely nothing to create a more positive and purposeful life, does it? The opposite happens.

The answer to this, was to "let this go" by allowing the light in. I do this by sitting still and visualizing light shining or raining down on me. I don't need to go through a whole ritual of lighting candles, putting on music, or whatever. I just do it. This process takes no more than 1 minute. For me, when I do this, the Light I surround myself with I interpret to be "higher information."

When I am in this state, I consider myself in higher information mode. These 101 Insights were written from this same mode. I think of myself downloading higher information that obliterates the "weight." It is a way of changing states. Be still and refuel.

Insight #93

EXPRESSING BEAUTY

Start to notice the beauty around you. Notice it in people, animals, bugs, and trees. This will assist you in creating more beauty in your life. See the beauty in everything. Express what you see to others. Write it. Make it art. Express it!

What in the world? Noticing beauty was not one of my fortes. I was not raised to see beauty. I was caught off guard by this Insight. This Insight suggests I begin to notice beauty around me. I'm not sure what beauty is.

I began by seeing the beauty in people. This was the easiest for me to do. I trained myself to look at people and no matter how weird, ugly, sad or angry they were, I forced myself to look at them as though they were beautiful. I would look at them from the outside and find something attractive. It might be their eyes, hair, or shoes. It didn't matter what it was, as long as I could see there was beauty on the person from the outside. After beauty on the outside is established, I would look for beauty on the inside. When I was with angry people, I found it easy to look at them and know they are angry because they are in fear of loss. Most anger comes from fear of loss. It's an odd yet empowering feeling looking at someone and no matter what he or she is saying or how he or she is behaving, you see beauty in them. It's very calming. It also makes it more difficult to be caught up in their "drama" because I look at the situation differently. The beauty in the person I see, allows me freedom to love them more.

Beauty in nature is a bit more difficult for me to see. Animals, bugs, and trees were a bit more difficult because they were so oblivious to me. I had to seek out beauty. Once sought, I found a new respect and a calming feeling. To me a tree is just a tree, but now I wonder how long that tree has stood. I wonder how many times it has been rained on. I wonder what trials Mother Nature herself has put this tree through, and yet the tree still stands. I admire the tree for laying down its roots and standing tall. This might all sound a bit silly, but by doing this, I learned a new respect for people, places, and nature. I learned a new respect for life.

Seeing beauty in people allows me to photograph people in a new way. If I am photographing a person who somewhat repels me, be it because of their physical appearance or their personality, I can go into that "find the beauty" mode. What previously may have had me photographing an obligatory functional photo session is now an opportunity to connect with the beauty in front of me. From my perspective, I am a better person and a better photographer because I can see the beauty in people.

Insight #94

BEAUTY

Imagine a place that is barren, devoid of life. Now imagine a place that is full of life, luscious greens, bountiful in flora and fauna. Bursting with energy. Which would you choose for yourself? Is too much beauty for you wrong? Know the more beauty you see, the more you create. Greed only takes place when beauty is for self-gratification. Beauty is meant to be shared!

I have to chuckle when I get Insights like this. The Insights must be on a beauty kick. Nature boy I am not. If I lived alone, I doubt I would even have a real plant in my home. I like fake ones, as they demand no attention other than the odd dusting.

For me, to begin seeing even more beauty than the previous Insight suggested, just seemed odd. Although I have been a photographer for many years, I rarely photograph landscapes, nature, and such. I am more into people, not pretty flowers, and sunsets.

It makes sense after reading this Insight that those pretty flowers, blue skies, greenery of grass and trees is far more appealing than say that of a concrete city. I began to look at nature and allow nature into my life. I began accepting nature. I began accepting nature as beauty. For some it may seem odd that I have to struggle to see the beauty in nature, but truly, I take the beauty of nature for granted. It is after this Insight I began to see beauty in other things like bicycles, cars, bridges, clothing, and especially the outdoors.

I realize beauty has been shut out of my life because it was "un-cool." Seeing beauty was not a masculine thing to do or be. As I allow myself to see beauty, life seems brighter. Imagine that! The more beauty I saw, the more beauty surrounded me. I allowed beauty in and beauty came to me. It is everywhere.

Now for the greed part. Beauty becomes greed, when the beauty we see or have is kept for ourselves. Beauty is meant to be shared. Shared could mean expressing it to another, "WOW! Did you see the color of the moon tonight?" The point is, when we see beauty or create beauty, it is meant to be shared. Sharing beauty energizes others. The energy is shared.

Insight #95

THE TREES

A forest has been created for you to see its beauty. It is a gift to be cared for. Stand beside a tree and send it light. Circle the tree, still sending it light. Sit beneath the tree and listen to the story of the tree. Each and every tree has its own story to share with you.

Ok. Ok. I have to say when I received this Insight I had to laugh. This is ridiculous. The trees have stories? What in the world has this to do with anything? I had just received the Seeing Beauty Insights, and now to have "trees" just seemed too much. I just can't see myself walking around trees and sending them light etc. It seems rather silly to me.

This Insight was written at a time when I was becoming aware of my surroundings. I was becoming aware of a life force. It is not really me to have much to do with nature. At the time of this writing, I was living (and still do) on the west coast of British Columbia, which is known for its oceans and trees. Yes, huge trees, mountains, lakes, and seawater surround me. Rather idyllic, yes? But for the most part, I never gave them much thought except when I leave the area and the world suddenly looks flat and boring.

I decided to drive to a remote part of Vancouver Island where the largest trees still reside and spend an evening there. I traveled with family and we set up our tents. Yes, I was camping. I prefer nice hotels but...there was nothing here but tall trees and bear poop.

In the morning, I went in search of the trees. I was still chuckling at the thought I was out here in a forest waiting to chat with trees. All the family joined in on this. The children seemed more able to grasp the concept of listening to trees than I did. We separated from each other and we all went to find "our" tree.

I have to admit, it was oddly intoxicating being in a quiet place of nature where I know phones aren't going to ring, the doorbell is not going to dong, there are no cars, no other distractions. I walked quietly and listened to my inner voice, my higher self, call it what you will, directing me to a large tree. I was still shaking my head in disbelief wondering what I was doing.

As instructed by the Insight, I began to send the tree light (no snickering), after all no one is going to see me right? So I sent the tree light, and walked around it encircling it as I went. Best to do this encircling with eyes open I quickly learned. As I sent energy out to the tree, and after walking completely around it while still giving it energy, I found myself feeling more energized as if the energy I gave the tree was returning to me.

I had the familiar feeling to pick up my pen and paper, so I did just that while sitting under the tree. As I wrote, it felt different, as though it wasn't my usual source of writings. At the risk of sounding too airy-fairy, it was as though the tree was speaking to me. The tree spoke of a great many things, none of which would interest you. The point being the tree had a story. Now where the heck does a tree get a story?

Methinks, perhaps I have been in the woods too long.:) Yet I tried this over and over, receiving a different energy, a different story from each tree. My wife and children returned after they each had found their own different tree. To my amazement, they too received stories. They had written words as though spoken from the tree. We listened as each one spoke of what their tree said to them. That night I lay awake. Not because I was thinking about trees, but because there was this damn bear sniffing around our tent. I think I like the city better.

Upon reflection and not being a scientist, the only reasoning I have that trees can tell a story is they absorb carbon dioxide or is it monoxide - that which we breathe out. Is it possible through exhaling our breath, our thoughts are transferred to the recipient... the trees, and through attuning to them; I picked up whatever they collected?

I don't really know, but it is the best theory I have at this time. So, if you get a chance find yourself a tree, encircle it with light, sit at the base, and listen for the story.

You might want to wait until there are no bears.

Insight # 96

FOOD

Eat light. Eat good foods. Energize your body.

My body is a machine. No more and no less. Within my body dwells my spirit or soul. It is important I keep my body as healthy as possible. An unhealthy body requires much energy to attempt to heal the weakness. This energy could be better spent elsewhere.

The best analogy I can give in regards to a healthy body is our bodies are like automobiles. Automobiles need constant maintenance and scheduled repairs along with the proper intake of fuel to run at maximum efficiency. If an automobile is neglected for too long it will have a breakdown. Some kind of maintenance will be required.

So it is for humans. My physical machine needs the correct amount of quality nourishment. I need to put good foods (not gasoline) into my body. I want to run like a finely tuned machine. My healthy body is far more capable of accessing higher thoughts than a body clogged with garbage and debris.

I energize my body by feeding it the right foods. I energize my body by allowing it to have the best sources of incoming physical energies it can have.

P.S. I have a weakness for Cheetos, Cheese Puffs, and well… a few others…Ok, lots of others.

Insight #97

STILL

It is easy when you become still enough to listen. There is in each one of us the little voice. That little voice can be the voice of the higher self, angels, the God within. When we choose to be still and just listen, it allows for hearing these higher forces.

When I need questions answered, being still, and listening often gives me insights I have never even thought before. We all have a higher self, a God within who does everything possible to assist us on our spiritual journey. I can tell you I do not like being still. It makes more sense to me to be active, to be doing something. I mostly feel solutions to my problems will come to me from doing something. I don't see how answers will come to me by being still. And yet, time and time again it is when I am still, when I have quieted the external and internal chatter I receive answers. It is that time when I am quiet, I can actually hear a solution or new way to look at a problem that allows me to chart a different course, take a different path. I can only imagine the frustration my God must feel when not all his talents, skills, and knowledge are utilized because I am just too darn noisy to listen.

I suppose one of the great challenges for me has been to discern between little voices of conscience vs. the little voice of God. I can best explain this (I hope) by saying the voice of conscience feels more like listening to my head. It feels more like logical thinking. It is as though I am accessing my internal database, searching through the past to come to a logical conclusion. I sort out pros and cons, the good, the bad, and make a choice. This is the conscience talking. I believe in the end, conscience becomes a battle between what I know to do and what I want to do. Conversely, being still and listening affords no battle between should and should not's. The head, although strangely quiet, has thoughts, new thoughts. Whereas the conscience goes to the past to decide the future, the stillness of listening to God thoughts, do not. As if by magic, although I certainly never consider listening to God a magic trick, the thoughts that arrive are of a higher nature. It's as though I wonder to myself why I never thought of that before, or tell myself I just received a really cool way of looking at a problem far above what my conscience ever could have come up with. God always plays win-win.

Being still is not about clearing the mind and sitting in a void. Staring at a candle and going blank for a while does honor the STILL, but other than a mental rest, serves no purpose. Being STILL is about asking important questions that allow the Guide to assist me in moving forward. It is about allowing higher energies to come in and actually to listen to them. Being still is listening for insights to important questions.

Insight #98

CONTROL

Know control only surfaces when there is fear of loss. By letting go of the fear of loss, you will find there is no need for control.

Fear of Loss. Fear of losing a relationship, money, power, security, love, and a host of other losses I can imagine. When I feel myself doing a control number or feeling someone is trying to control me, I look at the situation from a fear of loss point of view. I ask myself, what am I afraid of losing? In the case where I feel someone is controlling me, I ask myself, what is this other person(s) afraid of losing?

A person who insists on controlling a conversation is a person afraid of not being heard. A person who controls money is afraid of not having enough. A person who controls another with their force is afraid of being small. A person who controls a relationship is afraid of losing that relationship. A person who is controlling at work is afraid of not being valued or of being unemployed.

When I discover what the fear of loss is, it is easier to understand why my control program kicks into gear. If I control, I create what I fear. I actually manifest the very experience I am trying to avoid. The harder I try to control a person or situation the more it will manifest the way I did not want it to go. I think of relationships where one of the partners is so controlling from fear of loss they smother the partner with possessiveness. They keep tabs on their partner; they are in what seems like, constant communication. They are jealous of those the partner meets. They try to keep the partner to themselves so there is less chance of them leaving. In most cases, the partner eventually feels the lack of freedom, the intrusion of privacy and the clingy desperateness from their partner and they seek a way out. They usually find it, but not until after some serious emotional drama of arguing, fighting and bargaining. The controller in this case gets exactly what they feared (loss of love or loss of their partner). If fear had never existed, or if it had been dealt with, the chances of manifesting the loss may never have happened.

What I focus on having or not having is what I will have. In other words, wherever my focus is will be what my future will be. I must focus on what I want from a loving perspective rather than a fear perspective. I can create what I want from love not from fear. I choose never to have to use trickery, manipulation or force to receive.

Receiving from a place of love means there is no need for control. The energy of love (vs. control) allows manifestations to appear that support and uplift all involved. What I focus on, where I allow myself to dwell, where I take action, is what is and what will manifest for me. If my thoughts and actions are from fear of loss, I will lose. If my thoughts and actions are from love, I will win.

Insight #99

SCARCITY

Whenever there is lack of, a shortage, the answer is not to cut back or to cut out, but to create more. When you are stuck with not enough, it is a sure sign to create more. You have the power to create whatever you want.

Scarcity. In a business I co-owned with a group of partners, there took a downward financial spiral. Sales dropped due to a number of reasons. The economy changed, competition increased, management (yes me too) lacked the correct business skills, etc. etc. the reasons could go on and on and all are considered valid. We, the partners of the business, decided what we needed to do. Our fear of scarcity led us to make decisions to cut expenses. They were not easy decisions, especially since the cuts were generally labor cuts. We felt we had no choice but to let people go. We even cut our own salaries. We cut everything we thought we could cut to meet our goals. To many this would be good business practice, to bring expenses in line with income to continue to create the necessary profit for the business to continue. Ignorantly I watched, and reluctantly but willingly, participated in these cuts. To my surprise income of the business dropped even further and again we adjusted by making further cuts. We continued along this downward spiral. Emotions ran high between workers and management. Emotions became heated between management and management. Suddenly an entire business that was profitable a few months ago was now operating in an energy of scarcity panic.

No one thought to say, let's expand, let's create more, let's be creative about growth. No, we were all just too afraid to lose what we already had. It was not long before management became fractured and was reduced in size to such a point it was a further case of mismanagement rather than management. Shortly thereafter, the business went into receivership and eventually was sold by the receiver for outstanding debts. While I take ownership of my role in the failure of this business, I wonder if I had paid attention to this Insight, might I have turned it around?

At the time of writing this, I own my own business and I do listen to this Insight. When I feel scarcity, I tend to spend more. This drives my wife crazy, but I like the energy of creating and building rather than shrinking and squeezing. I no longer go into fear of loss when scarcity starts staring at me. I go into full production, creation mode, to think of new ways of doing business to continue that income flow.

Many corporations are downsizing. They are becoming lean and mean. While I believe fiscal and financial responsibility is part of any business, the idea of cutting back because of a belief there is not enough to go around will surely create the same. How can a company preach financial abundance when everything about them says they are scared silly of losing what they have?

If I felt scarcity in love, would I choose to snip out some love to get more? Should I downsize my love, thinking somehow by doing this I am being responsible? If I felt scarcity in love, should I take stock and remove those people who are expendable so I can keep what love I do have? Can I create a profit of love while shrinking the amount of love I am willing to give out? I think not.

Scarcity comes from fear of loss. "I won't have enough." "I better hold on to what I have, at least that is better than having nothing." This is called holding on to moldy peanuts. Let the moldy peanuts go and be open to receiving fresh ones.

How can one create when one is in fear-of-loss mode? You cannot. The only way to remove scarcity in your life, whether it is money, love, sex, joy, peace, etc. is to create it. If it is missing, you get to create it. How will you create more of what is missing in your life? Not from fear or fear of loss, I hope.

Create by being open to receiving. Create by removing the beliefs that prevent you from having all you want. Give! In an area where you find scarcity, give more. That sounds ironic, doesn't it? But, the more you give in an area where there is scarcity, the more will come back to you. Give from the heart knowing as you give you are creating your own abundance.

So it is for all scarcity. Scarcity is neither bad, nor good, it just is. It is what I have created. If I do not like the areas in my life where there is scarcity, I have to change it. I am the only one who has the power to change my reality.

That reminds me of a joke I heard. A poor man prays every night that he would win the lottery. One night he gets a visit from God who says he will win the lottery within the year.

Three months go by and still this man has not won the lottery; however, he is not worried, he heard and believed what God told him.

Six months go by and still no winnings. He is beginning to get a little worried and boy, he sure could use the money.

Nine months go by and this man is getting very worried.

A year goes by and the man does not win the lottery. In a fit of frustration and rage he screams out to God, "You promised me! You promised me I would win the lottery!" To which God replies, "The least you could have done is buy a ticket."

Humorous yes, but what a truth lies in that joke.

Scarcity is not a punishment. Scarcity is just a messenger telling me I need to look at and clean up an area in my life. Scarcity of any kind can be overcome. When I feel scarcity, I can choose to **give more**, to **create more** in that area.

Insight #100

INTENTION

To walk blindly is not always the wisest decision. The intention of what you are asking for is all-important. For that is what you will create. This is what will manifest. To have no intention is also an intention and leaves you open to be blown around. A time of chaos may follow. Be clear on your intention. Today I intend to_____.

Definition of Intention: A plan of action, either immediate or ultimate.

It is from my intention that all things manifest. To intend to go to point B from point A will surely result in arriving at point B. There must be an action for me to arrive at point B from point A. If I intend to arrive at point B, at some point I must take **action**.

Let us say point B is a football game. I intend to arrive there. I have intention. Intention without action is not intention. I took the action by getting in my car, driving through traffic, handled any personal obligations, ensured I had enough money, parked my vehicle and walked to the field. That is intention with action. Not everyone who arrives at this same game took the same action. Some of them walked, while others rode the bus. Some people rode the train or subway. No matter how they arrived, they all had intention to arrive at the game. It is intention combined with action that produces the desired results.

And so it is in our lives. Wherever we are in our lives, is based upon our intentions or lack of them. Everything we have is from intention.

Everything we do not have is from lack of intention. To walk forward without intention leaves me to become a victim. If I have intention but no action, I am in a place of wishful thinking. While thinking and visualizing are great tools and important steps, only by adding ACTION does the wishful thinking become reality.

If I make all choices by intention and no action, I will not arrive at my intention. I will arrive somewhere, but not at point B where I intended to go.

I am clear about my intentions. Intentions are not wishful thinking.

I only make intentions upon which I plan to take action.

Insight #101

TREASURES

Are you willing to share your treasures? When you share your treasures, you will receive more treasures. The greatest treasures are those of the heart. Your treasures are worthy of being seen.

Throughout this book, I have spoken of the gifts we all have. All of us have gifts that when shared lead us to a place of inner harmony and fulfillment. As we reach the last Insight, I am reminded we all have our treasures.

My treasures have no value if they are buried within. My treasures need to be brought out. My treasures need to be shown. My treasures need to be shared. When my treasures are shared, they bring value to the person sharing and the person receiving.

It is within our hearts we will find the greatest treasures. There, in the warmth of our soul, lie treasures so profound, so wonderful, so uplifting, when brought forth, when shared, they change the lives of all who are so touched.

It is inside the heart where special treasures lie. It is the place of my inner knowing, my inner desire. I have known what my treasure is for a long time. I have always wanted, and still want, to help people. I wanted to help everyone only I was not passionate to any of the avenues that help people. I did not want to be part of the health scene. Not because I don't approve of the health society, where it seems every body part and every disease has its own foundation, I just don't feel attracted to it. I have little interest in politics except for wondering when politicians will stop bickering and begin serving. I have little interest in our environment. I know, I Know that is just politically incorrect and while I certainly approve of any changes to better our environment I am not attracted to it in such a way that has me expending energy towards it. I liken this non-choosing as similar to being at a high school dance and surrounded by wonderful young girls' each of them I would look at, but with which one do I really want to dance? Which one makes my heart go "ping"?

What I have been and still am attracted to, is the wonderment of people letting go of their restricting past, moving forward, having breakthroughs. At one point, I said to myself and with conviction too, "My life purpose is to rid the world of emotional pain." It was years later I realized I did not have that power. Not because I was weak or lacked courage, but because I don't have the power to remove anyone's pain. The only person who can remove one's pain is himself or herself. I had to re-choose. I get excited when I see, through communicating with people, they begin to see they have a way out of hopelessness and despair. I become moved when those around me get out of the rut they are in. I want people to know they can change their reality; they do have a purpose - they can love and they can be loved.

For many, the heart has been dormant far too long. It is time to awaken your treasures. It is time to realize your treasures, your gifts, are worthy of being seen. Share your treasures with others and know as you do, an abundance of love, inner peace and joy will find its way to you and others in ways never expected. **For when you share your treasures, *miracles happen*.**

Conclusion

As I mentioned in my introduction it has been many years since I received the 101 Insights. While I may have decided to write them in a book to share them with you, I found as I wrote them I learned even more from them. Most of the Insights still speak to me in my current life situation. I wonder if I have grown spiritually and emotionally, I say yes, but after writing and reading the Insights over many times, I still realize I have a long way to go.

I hope this book has offered you some inspiration to move forward, to be more loving, and to allow yourself to be loved more. People ask me what is my favorite Insight. That is a hard choice. Yet, if I were forced to answer, I would have to say it is a toss-up between two Insights. They are "Forgiveness of Self" and "Forgiveness." These two Insights have had the biggest impact. Forgiveness of self and others is so empowering, so freeing, so uplifting that while all the other Insights have value (still not sure about the Trees Insight), the Forgiveness Insights rise above the others.

There are two more books I have in my head. As of yet I have not had the energy raising experience of the 101 Insights. Still, I can't deny I will write a book called 101 Spiritual Insights and 101 Relationship Insights.

Of course, they will not be written unless I have intention with action.

Please take a moment to visit my website at http://www.101insights.com

Thanks for having the intention and taking the action to read The 101 Insights.

Phil Walmsley